Chasing Happiness

A Novel by

Kaitlyn Jones

Chasing Happiness

Depression does not get up and leave one day – it is
a constant struggle, but a battle worth fighting.

Chasing Happiness

A Novel by

Kaitlyn Jones

Prologue

It was finally my birthday; I was officially 19 years old. We took the LRT downtown, just Irvine and I, for a special dinner in the Calgary Tower. On the way home, I looked out the window into the darkened roads and I thought of the night I rode a camel out into the desert near Pushkar, India with my tour group: we had our dinner made there, in the middle of nowhere, while a couple of traditional fire dancers performed for us. We sat in a line, which I had made sure to be at the end so I could leave regularly to smoke my fresh pack of cigarettes. I enjoyed the time alone in the dark behind the small shelter where they had cooked the spicy meal for us. I looked up to the stars and realized I had never seen so many.

The air was colder further away from the fire, and it almost felt like home. It had reminded me of a nice night I had spent with my ex-boyfriend in Ontario during an outdoor concert, and how we laid on the grass looking at the stars listening to the live music from afar.

In the dark, I stood alone behind the shelter, and listened to the group giggle and cheer. I then had a flashback to getting on the bus leaving Jaipur earlier on this trip: I sat by myself at first, and the only person who showed interest in my company was the tour guide, but he was just doing his job. I noticed, as I stood in the darkened desert, that I had not made any friends on this tour – which in all honesty was my normal – but I began to feel the weight of all the times I've ever been alienated from a group without explanation.

My mind dug deeper, and everything started to pour down on me: memories of all the times I was just awkwardly there, with nothing to say and no one to confide in. I thought of all the times I have watched two strangers become friends so easily, and how I still have never been able to figure it out. I remembered being bullied in elementary school for being too skinny and quiet. I recollected the feeling of being numb and hurting myself just to feel something.

I remembered being picked on by an old friend in high school, and losing touch with all our mutual friends, until I had no one left. I remembered locking myself in the washroom on the third floor of that high school during lunch breaks and fighting back tears. I remembered the feeling of starting a new school in Alberta, not knowing anyone, and not knowing where to sit or what to do during our breaks. I recalled the feeling of having one of my ex-boyfriends put his hands around my neck and call me horrible names; feeling so helplessly weak and unable to protect myself. I thought of how I was refused to be promoted to become a team leader at work just because I did not fit in socially with the management team. I remembered the feeling of being just another booty-call whenever *he* wanted. I remembered all the low moments in my life, and all the overwhelming feelings that were attached.

There on the train sitting beside Irvine after our beautiful meal together, I was frozen in this darkened mindset and I couldn't move my body.

Irvine lightly shook my hand, and the present came flushing back. I focused on our reflection in the window. I saw how uncertain and lost I looked, then I saw my knight in shining armor beside me. He looked at me concerned and said, "you're not alone". I turned to him and kissed his lips.

"Thank you." I whispered, looking deeply into his eyes.

Chapter One

My brother had told me before I left that he expected a wild story after I came back because "you always seem to do something crazy while you're on your own". Which was ultimately true: I was not the same person when I traveled, especially when I traveled alone, because I always said yes.

I had a smile on my face when I landed in Dehradun. The sun was already setting when I walked out of the plane and onto the pavement towards the airport. It took about 12 seconds to stride from the backside of the airport to the front exit where a group of taxi drivers stood, holding their signs. I approached them, searching for my name as if it were a game. I was pleasantly surprised to find my name – and subsequently my driver – with ease, and then we headed to a white taxi car nearby. I threw my bigger backpack in the trunk, and held onto my small blue day pack, as this had most of my valuables.

We drove down a zigzagged road, swerving in and out of the passing lane to overcome cars and motorcyclists. I noticed my seatbelt had nothing to latch itself into, so I swayed side to side with the car. I leaned back and let myself relax, reminding myself that Indian drivers were the best drivers I have experienced. I pressed the nail of my index finger into my thumb and tried to focus on my smile, as I quickly became nauseous.

The driver's almost constant honking took me back to countless memories all flooding in at once: from sitting in the taxi with Karen after finding her at the waiting area in the Manila Airport, to driving through the streets of Mumbai almost 3 years ago. I smiled to myself: *this is why I love Asia.*

I looked around at the dark surroundings and tried to soak in this moment. *This is it: finally you are back.* I thought about how long I have wanted to come back to this incredible country, and how I should be so excited, but instead I found myself at my usual neutral and numb state. Nothing surprised, excited, scared or intrigued me. I was just there with an empty head. This is how I've spent most of my adult life after fighting for years to let go of my toreros mind – the mind that kept me up all night shaming me for the things I did and those I did not have the courage to do. I finally came back to India in search of a little bit of happiness.

This had been the country where I had experienced true, absolute, unconditional happiness almost three years ago: a simple hour of bliss dancing in some nightclub with my tour group. Besides my age, my life had not really changed all that much from that time: I was fresh out of school and started working full time at a job. The biggest difference was that I had been sober since January 1st of this year.

We turned onto a busy road, which I quickly prepared myself to be my neighbourhood for the next month, but the driver just kept on going. I tried to remember how long the drive was as per what the website had said.

We weaved through pigs, donkeys, dogs, monkeys, and humans

walking on the sides of the road. We went up a slope on the other side

of the town and began doing switchbacks up the mountain. We left

the lights and the crowded streets behind, following a twisting road

and the red lights of a car ahead of us. I wondered how far we were

going to go.

After driving in the dark, for what seemed to be half an hour of me

nodding in and out of my tiredness, we finally headed into another

sea of lights and stores. I looked at all the people walking around in

search for the best deals and restaurants as we passed by.

Suddenly he turned the car around, stopping in front of a statue,

then opened the trunk and stepped outside to greet a young boy who

blended in with the scenery behind him. I grabbed my small bag,

stepped outside, and prepared myself to take my large bag – which

was only 12 pounds, but my back was sore from my travels. The

young boy had acne scars on his cheeks and wide eyes. He grabbed my backpack before I could, and he slung it over his back. He asked the driver something which I assumed was "that's it?" and the driver laughed, pointing his hand to the car, while I imagined he explained that that is all I came with.

I have tried to learn a great deal about body language while traveling, especially in Asia. I would follow along with conversations, trying to understand what was happening before someone would either translate or decide I did not need to know.

Without words, I followed the boy down some steps and towards the bridge I had seen on social media. On the side just before entering onto the bridge, there was a man roasting some sort of nut, and the aroma took me back to Makati City where street vendors roasted nuts for anyone who passed by. The smell carried so many memories walking down the streets in the Philippines; my heart cried out to go back there.

There were monkeys on the side of the bridge, and I became uneasy when we got close to them. I had been frightened by similar monkeys at a temple consumed by a gang of them in Indonesia. I knew they weren't shy and would become violent easily.

We walked through, letting motorcyclist priority because their honking was just intolerably loud. I was smiling the whole way as we squeezed past the beggars, the tourists and two bulls. I quietly said to myself: "I miss this".

From time to time the boy would check over his shoulder to see if I were still following him. I followed closely behind because the circumstances deterred me from walking beside him. We turned right at a statue at the other end of the bridge, and followed a road full of shops, where I saw a ton of scarves for sale, piquing my interest. I started to reflect on the fact that I had no idea who the statues we saw were of – I had no prior knowledge of any Hindu Gods beside

Ganesh. This month would be a great chance for me to deepen my

knowledge.

More food was cooking on the sides of the street, where the staff

knew the aroma was the best way to attract customers into their

restaurants.

We took a quick turn left down a narrow alleyway, which quickly

climbed uphill. I carefully stepped over a small green snake that just

wanted to go to the other side of the alley. I watched my step to be

sure not to step in cow dung as well.

How would I have found this myself? I am so relieved I scheduled a

taxi with the school. I would have never found this place at this time of

night, carrying my backpacks and without any data on my phone.

We turned right, then went quickly up a few stairs that led us

immediately to the front desk of the school. I told my name to a man

with medium-length curly hair and a big smile which made his eyes become *Chinito*. He told me to put my bags behind the desk and go

upstairs for the welcoming ceremony.

"Nah, that's alright, I don't mind." I had expected to be late and

miss the welcoming ceremony all together, but the man insisted, and

then the boy showed me up several stairs. I had to take my shoes off at

the last room at the top of the stairs, and I was embarrassed because I

knew my socks smelled terrible after over 24 hours of travel.

I walked in to see everyone standing in a circle around the fire. I

could see myself from the perspective of the others in the circle, who

had made it on time and were already adjusted to their surroundings.

I joined the circle beside an older man and a middle-aged woman.

Everyone clapped slowly to the rhythm and there was a local man

dressed nicely who sang a chant. He was handsome. Some of the

people attempted to follow along with his singing. I was quickly given

a bowl with a fire lit inside and was signaled to come into the center of the circle to move the bowl around the other fire in the middle, then pass it along.

We eventually sat down, and I noticed I was the only one without a red dot on my forehead. I felt a surge of satisfaction rush over me, as if I were proud of everyone here to be experiencing this. I did not feel embarrassed to be the only one that didn't attend the whole ceremony; I felt like it was everyone's turn in this room to feel this ritual spiritually and have their time to feel special.

There were a few more teachers there, who sat comfortably along the same wall as me. I could only focus on a small woman who spoke quickly. The men beside her got up and gave each of us a folder that contained a pencil, a notebook, a textbook and a small paper pamphlet which said: "Prayer & Mantrajapa".

They also gave us a thick orange book that read: "Asana Pranayama Mudra Bandha". I quickly flipped through the pages and saw graphics depicting yoga poses with explanations and benefits.

I looked around the circle which was oddly shaped – with one long line facing the teachers, and then a sudden curve towards the wall behind me, where people clustered trying to find room to see the teachers.

I saw a young woman in dreadlocks sitting across the circle to my left. I was taken aback – she was stunning. I envied her natural glow.

The small woman who commanded the room, instructed us to introduce ourselves, say where we came from and what our expectation was while we were here. Immediately I knew I only had one goal while I was here – to be happy. I carefully listened to everyone – especially the girl with the dreadlocks.

She sat almost in front of a young man with long hair and a relaxed

expression. When he spoke, it was as if all the stress in the room had

fallen asleep. They both said they were from Canada, and I assumed

that they were a couple. There were only a handful of guys here,

which was a relief for the part of me that had to tell Irvine about my

classmates, but I knew deep down, I was not able to make girlfriends

easily, and I would want to be around the boys.

Everyone in the room did not look like strangers – there was a

familiar presence about them all. I felt a warmness towards everyone,

and I was happy that they were experiencing this.

Once the ceremony ended, I headed downstairs to grab my bag.

The young boy who brought my bag was there waiting for me. He

picked up my bag from behind the desk and took me back down the

alleyway where we came, but quickly stopped at a glass door where he

spoke with another young man behind the desk. Both boys then

walked me to my room on the third floor. The hotel boy unlocked the door and gave me the key, then the other boy put my backpack on my

bed. They left quickly without saying anything.

I realized I had to unpack now, but I was tired from traveling and

not sleeping in a bed in the past two days.

I looked at myself in the mirror: neither excited nor sad.

I brushed off the thought of "*why aren't I phased?*" and assumed I

was too tired to be emotional right now.

I opened the metal wardrobe in the room and started pulling out the

plastic storage bags of clothes I had organized in my backpack for

optimal packing space and efficient retrieval. I did not remove the

clothes from the bags, instead I took out my toiletries which were in a

plastic travel bag that you could get at the airport, and I brushed my

teeth then washed my face. I laid on the bed, realizing it was stiff and

the blankets were thin. I knew it was going to be a rough sleep, but

thankfully I was tired from the travels.

Earlier at the ceremony we had to split into two groups – one group

who would have a Vinyasa class in the morning for two hours, and

then Hatha later at night for two hours; the other group's schedule

was vice versa. I had chosen Vinyasa first thing in the morning,

because I knew that sweating was the best way to start the day. It

would release endorphins and make me feel good, and I wanted that

feeling for the rest of this month.

Chapter Two

I was wide awake at 4 AM, only to go to class at 6 AM. I filled the

bucket in the washroom with warm water and proceeded to lather

myself then rinse off the soap by using a smaller plastic sauce pot-

looking item – which I knew as a *tabo* from my time in the

Philippines.

Written on the schedule was "tea and fruits at 5:30 AM", and so I

walked over to the school in the dark. The wind was strong, and I was

freezing cold. The alleyway was narrow and abandoned, but the

entrance of the school was lit up and open. I hoped it would get

warmer during my stay here, because I did not bring any warm

clothes.

There were a few girls in the room already, drinking tea and eating

bananas. I was not hungry, but I ate a banana because our breakfast

was not until 10 AM. I sat there, trying to focus on the conversations and perhaps try to include myself. The conversations were all the

same:

 "How did you sleep?"

"Good, how did you sleep?"

"Pretty good."

I would rather say nothing at all then to go through a useless

conversation like that, but I knew these first points of contact were

how friendships were made. I was briefly engaged by a woman that I

assumed spoke German due to her accent. I smiled as we all got up to

go to the classroom above, as I had remembered the handful of

German travelers I met along my own adventures, and how I always

got along with them more than anyone else. Our class was to be held

in the same room where the welcome ceremony was held last night. It

was noticeably colder here compared to the room we had just left. It

was dark, and we could not hear anyone talking over the wind that gusted through the loosely fitted windows. There were two walls that

held old windows from the ceiling to my waist, and it looked like if I

pushed one fitted glass, they would all break away.

Collectively we did not know how to set up the room, as the teacher

had not placed their mat to display the front of the class.

The room had an upside down "L" shape, and we decided that the

short part to the right would be where the teacher stood. I was in the

back row in the corner furthest from the door. I sat down shivering.

The only pants and sweater I had with me were the ones I wore on the

plane yesterday, and so I wore only capris.

While everyone still adjusted their mats, a curly blonde woman sat

down in an office chair to the side of the appointed "front of the

room".

"You guys chose an odd direction; most classes face this wall." She made some gestures with her hands to suggest we were sideways. If we moved, I would have been at the front left side of the classroom.

I thought she was a student at first, but she stayed there and continued to speak. She did not command the room, but we respected her. I admired her hair – it reminded me of a friend from my childhood: it wasn't perfectly curly, but wavy with some curls within.

We didn't practice any movements today. She took us through our textbook and what was expected of us for the month. I realized I had put myself back into school. I had mixed emotions, as school has been such a dreadful experience for me throughout my whole life, but I knew this was no ordinary school.

This was our daily schedule (with an excursion on Sundays and Thursdays having only Vinyasa and Hatha classes):

6:00 – 7:00 Vinyasa Yoga

7:15 – 8:15 Vinyasa Yoga

Self-Study Block

9:00 – 10:00 Pranayama

10:00 – 11:00 Breakfast

11:00 – 12:00 Philosophy

12:00 – 13:00 Anatomy

13:00 - 14:30 Lunch

Self-Study Block

17:00 – 18:45 Hatha Yoga

19:15 – 20:15 Meditation

20:30 Dinner

We fixed our mats for our second Vinyasa teacher – I moved to the other side of the room into the small addition, and although technically still in the front row, I was off to the side so there was no one behind me.

After our class, I went back to my room to shower again and warm up.

I went early to our next class because I did not know where it would be held – the schedule said, "Hotel Ganga View Hall". I asked a guy who looked like he was lost too. We went up the stairs to the fourth floor of our school, looking on each level for a mysterious room to appear. Once we reached the top floor and no one was there, we headed back down, asking another student where it was once we got to the lobby. We crossed the alleyway to a hotel just in front of our school, then walked up the stairs to the fourth floor where we found a large room with blue carpet and blue ceiling panels. We were panting our way up, trying to wrap our heads around the fact that we would have to climb these stairs at least two times a day plus the stairs in our school three to four times if we ate the provided meals.

Philosophy was a subject I did not expect to learn for a yoga course, but I knew it would become my favourite class once the teacher

started to speak. He spoke slowly, thinking about what he would say –
not because of the translation, but you could tell he wanted to find the
best words to express himself. He was calm and knowledgeable.

The next class was Anatomy, taught by a shy guy who was obviously
overqualified to be teaching the basics. This class reminded me of my
interest in biology during high school, and I hoped to remember what
I learned – even if it felt like a lifetime ago.

For the first couple of days at the school, I ate the provided
breakfast and lunch with most of the students. I would skip dinner
because I was barely awake during evening meditation and needed to
adjust to this time-zone and our busy schedule. I bought some chips
at a convenience store just beside the school, to fill my urge to munch
on something before I sleep. I lost a lot of weight quickly from not
eating three meals a day – on top of four hours of yoga practice. My
last meal would be at 13:30, then I wouldn't eat until 10:00 the next
day. I knew this was not good, because when I did eat, I could never

finish the small portions I scooped up for myself. I knew previously I was not a big eater: normally I would eat like six times a day but very little portions.

In class I sat by myself, at a considerable distance from anyone else. I was always early, and no one ever laid their mat beside me – even if I was in the second row, there was always a gap. I quickly learned my lesson and proceeded to stay at the back of the room, where I could move around my mat and adjust my sitting position often without distracting others. Surprisingly, it was a huge adjustment to be sitting on the floor with no support. My back ached from trying to sit up straight.

I tried to keep my chin up and not to be bothered by not *fitting in* during classes, but it sunk in deep during our three-hour self study block after lunch: I was always by myself. I just sat alone in my room, doing my laundry in the bucket or on my bed watching comedy clips to take my focus away from the present and into a fantasy. The days were long – they always have been – and I wished for an escape.

On Saturday we had a Mantra Meditation class – we were in the fire ceremony classroom and it was the same handsome man who performed that first day. He had drums and bells, and he sat there at ease while everyone made a large circle to face him. We sat on the orange body pillows that were worn down from the sweat and use of countless students before us. I sat at the left side because the back was full already.

The teacher began to sing and teach us mantras. He would sing a line, then we would repeat it. We didn't really understand what we were saying, but eventually we got the hang of it.

He encouraged us to stand up and dance inside the circle of body pillows. Collectively, we all looked around at each other immediately, trying to find permission from everyone else to move our own bodies.

Suddenly, by chance, the lights went out due to a power outage –

which was very familiar to us after our time being here already. The

darkness liberated the class to dance freely and disregard any inner

thoughts of judgement. I stood at the back and clapped: I didn't feel at

ease. At this moment I wished I could have been high. I wanted to

dance, but my mind couldn't let my body be free.

After the Mantra Meditation, I vowed not to do that class next week.

I felt very uncomfortable. It reminded me of something in my past

that I could not clearly pin-point. All I knew was that deep down I did

not like it and so I gave myself permission not to go through it again.

The next morning was our first Sunday excursion, and we all

waited in the lobby of the school. I sat down on the couch before it

got busy, but then everyone who arrived stood in a group with their

backs towards me. The girls to my left, who sat on the other couches,

were speaking another language that I was unfamiliar with. The lobby

got crowded and I looked up at the security camera behind the desk that faced into this area and wondered if this room looked exactly

how it felt. I was just in the middle, surrounded by people, and yet I

was still alone. I tried looking around, to see if there was a

conversation I could easily slide into, but I ended up just looking

down at my hands. My fingernails were getting long now.

Eventually we all walked through the roads and across the bridge.

Everyone in front of me were in pairs. I tried to focus on my energy –

it had only been three days since I had arrived, and yet I felt extremely

relaxed and at peace. I felt connected to my body and to the earth

itself. I felt grounded. It was nice to just let go and not have to plan

anything – I would be living here for a month with everything already

scheduled for me. I had nothing to worry about and I could finally

focus on taking care of myself.

We took the stairs up to an opening where the statue I saw the first

night was. I looked at the statue, trying to memorize the detail, but it

didn't seem too notable or relatable – it was a young man holding a bow with arrows on his back. I forgot to take a look at the statue on the other side of the bridge, where the intersection was always overwhelmingly busy.

We got into jeeps that were waiting for us at the statue. We proceeded out of the town, driving for roughly an hour on dirt road. When we finally stopped, we found ourselves at the side of the road beside an abandoned building and a small vendor stall where three men sat chatting. I was glad to get out of the jeep, as the road was bumpy, and my stomach was uneasy. After all the jeeps arrived and everyone got out, we walked down the steps past a building that had a list of rules written in paint on the wall facing the trail that led downhill. We stopped as a group for a moment to read the English side, then continued down.

I looked at the sun coming through the trees and how it illuminated the leaves. Suddenly I felt at home: it was like a warm fall day before all the leaves turned their colour, and I walked with my mom on one of the many trails we have explored around Ontario. I watched the beautiful details in the leaves as I looked for the right picture to take. I saw a branch that reached out, framed by the green leaves, and I knew that was the shot. I slowed down in an attempt to bring myself at the end of our line, but there were too many people and my social anxiety kicked in. I decided I would have the chance later to take that photo, and to not make a scene, I carried on with the group.

We passed what I assumed to be a homestay for anyone coming here to meditate in the cave. There were a few cows – a mother and two babies – in the dirt lawn between the path we took and the homestay. There was also an outside kitchen island for the stove, sink and extra countertop, which was a common thing to see in Asia: it was a smart way to keep the smells out of the rest of your house.

I slid my flip-flops off and headed into the cave with the German guy I had been walking beside. We didn't say much as we both ducked into the dark cave. There was an open space where the sunlight barely came in, but it led into a smaller area where no light entered from outside. There were about six tourists there, who looked at us as we entered.

There was a shrine with some lit candles and incense burning. I sat down facing away from the tourists and closed my eyes. A couple more people trickled in, and some people left. It fell silent between bursts here and there, and I could hear my stomach moving, people swallowing and breathing. It was not what I imagined.

I held my eye closed and tried to focus on my breathing, but I was unable to enter a meditative state. I got up and walked outside – letting someone who waited in the open space near the entrance to have my spot.

I slipped my flip-flops back on and headed to the Ganga River in front of the homestay. There were a few concrete steps and then it was a vast shore of rocks for about 40 feet until the river. I eventually took my flip-flops back off to allow more grip on my steps. I moved slowly: balancing and connecting with each rock. I planted each foot, making sure it was secure, but every step felt like a dance; my movement was flowing and effortless. My steps were in rhythm and didn't feel awkward or wary. It felt like I was being carried in a flow state similar to when I used to do my martial arts katas. I reached an area away from anyone else, where I sat on the most perfect boulder. I crossed my legs and looked across the river. The lush jungle on the other side reminded me of all the animals that lurked in the thick vegetation. I had heard stories of tigers walking the streets near our school.

I put my bag down and wrapped myself in my new scarf that wore the colours green, yellow, red and a little bit of sky blue. I was starting to feel the image I wanted to project to others – I wanted to be a hippie.

I closed my eyes and brought my awareness to here and now. I took a few long breaths to center my mind, and easily began meditating. I enjoyed the sounds of the river just below me, close enough that if I reached my foot down, I could touch the water. It hummed beside me, almost in echo of "om".

The light danced through the trees across the river and flicked through my closed eyelids. There were tourists on the bridge down the way whose faint voices carried down-stream. My heart was open and vibrant, my mind was clear and present. I felt at peace, truly. I knew I had to be here, on this rock, on this gorgeous day. It felt like it was written already.

I later opened my eyes and watched the water maneuver around the rocks on the shore. I looked around, thinking I had been there a very long time, and everyone had left without me. I squinted my eyes until I could recognize the figure of some of the student's down-stream taking group photos together.

I decided I wanted to capture this moment of surreal calmness and took out my camera. I positioned it between some rocks, pointing the lens up toward where I would sit on my newfound rock. I put a timer and sat there. The first few shots would be to figure out the focus, so I wasn't blurry. I ran back and forth, and I noticed I got carried away. My feet started to hurt from the insensible steps I was taking to capture this fake scene. I had become obsessed with this photo that I lost my connection to the nature around me. I had become self-absorbed. I accepted my sore feet as a sign that I should stop. I collected my bag and flip-flops and walked towards the group.

On the way, my steps were awkward, and I lost my balance frequently – it was as though this was not the path I should have been taking. Inside of me, I knew there was only disappointment and sadness in front of me and the pathway was hard and uncertain.

My way to that perfect boulder was so smooth and secure, but now I felt like I was fighting the tide.

I didn't get too close to anyone, and I tried to find another perfect boulder to sit on. I found an awkward small one that was rough, but close enough to the water that I could wash my feet while waiting for everyone to be finished with their photoshoot. There was a man who came to bathe in the river just a few feet away from me. His offering to the Ganga River floated away and directly to where my feet were. Displeased, I washed the flower pedals off and stood up recalling the picture of the branch I wanted to take. I walked back towards the cave holding my flip flops so that my feet could dry off properly.

Passing the cows, I badly wanted to take a picture of them, but their owner watched me. I had a weird assumption that he would ask for money in exchange for the liberty to take photos of his animals. I walked back up the trail and found the perfect angle. Before I could get the right settings on my camera, I heard behind me: "Kaitlyn?" and I turned around.

It was the man with long hair who had greeted me on my arrival

day. He was walking with a young boy I had seen around the school.

"What are you doing here? Did you go to the cave? Did everyone

leave?"

"I just wanted to take some pictures." I shyly replied.

"Come down with us and we will find the group." he said invitingly.

"I will." I smiled.

I waited for them to pass and I took a few pictures. I slowly walked

down, looking for more photo opportunities. The owner of the cows

watched me as I stopped at the baby cow, and he came closer. I

looked at him and smiled, then I saw his hand reach out with his palm

to the sky. I then smiled at the ground as I continued to walk past

him. I had no money to give him, and I felt bad because I held an expensive camera in front of him, but truth be told he probably sees a

lot of tourists pass by.

The two men from the school turned around and the man with

long curly hair waved for me to join them, but I just smiled and

nodded, continuing my pace. I eventually followed them back to the

river, where everyone was.

I sat by the water again, which numbed my feet with its glacier

purity. Something inside of me felt like I was healing my feet from

earlier, but I brushed it off because I knew it came from my

preconceptions of the Ganga Holy River.

Chapter Three

The storm last night had taken away our Wi-Fi and electricity for the whole day. Thankfully, we had backup lights for the room and attached bathroom. I decided to check my photos from today, of me on my boulder, so I put my memory card into my phone. I realized I did not have the proper tool to stick into the hole to remove the memory card slot, but I did have a pen. It worked to get it open, and I put the memory card into the slot, then I slid it back into my phone. I opened the files to check the pictures, but nothing popped up. I knew the card must have adjusted out of the slot enough that it was unrecognizable by my phone. I grabbed the pen and poked the hole, but instead of pulling the slot out, the pen came out leaving the tip inside the hole. The ink spilled out and I was unable to remove it with my nails.

I had another pen, but I knew if this didn't work, I wouldn't have any pens to write with for the rest of the month: so, I grabbed my tweezers. I tried removing the pen top. I put my phone down a couple

times, trying to leave it and let this obsession go, but I could not stop

thinking about it. I became infatuated. I used the tweezers to scrape

the plastic coating on the side, and I pressed around the slot trying to

create some leverage to pull it up from the side. I was so irritated. I

just wanted the memory card back.

I grabbed a staple from the Prayer & Mantrajapa booklet we were

given for class. I managed to get it stuck in the pen top, and finally

remove that from the hole. However, when I used the staple to press

down and unlock the slot, it was still unsuccessful. I tried using the

staple around the side where I have carved a small dent, but it bent

too easily.

I threw my phone across the room. I wanted to smash it until the

slot fell out, returning my memory card. Suddenly I had an awareness

that if I broke my phone, I wouldn't be able to speak with Irvine, so I

got up to check if it was still working.

My perspective of this moment changed, as I reached down for my phone. I realized how crazy I had been, so much so that I wanted to cry out of frustration. I put my phone under my pillow and tried to forget about it.

On the porch, I dragged one of my chairs and a book that I had brought with me. I read there until I saw two men on a porch nearby looking over at me. Irritated, I went inside and showered, slowly getting ready for class. I stood under the warm water and let my sight get unfocused. I tried to remove myself from this moment, as if numbing myself from reality. This whole week I had been tested: I thought coming here I would finally find people like me but once again I was alienated. I thought I would finally meet people who instantly became my friends, and we would share a connection that I would remember for the rest of my life. Instead, I was alone.

I saw loneliness as the test: it was my biggest weakness. I let it dig in too deeply – enough that the painful emptiness inside broke me down every three months or so.

I guess it doesn't matter where I go, I'll never find someone who wants to be my friend.

I knew I sounded childish, but I had dealt with this loneliness since my third year of high school. Friendship was the only thing missing from my life, based off of Maslow's Hierarchy of Needs Theory: I knew who I was and what I succeeded in; I was loved by Irvine and my family; I felt security at home and wherever I went, and I had my most basic needs – food, water, a roof over my head and a warm bed. Friendship has always felt unnatural to me.

I have always hated the word "friend" because it was something I envied.

I never understood how people could trust each other so quickly.

To blindly associate yourself with someone before knowing who they

are. I always preferred to watch people interact with others to see

what kind of person they are. If they are quick to gossip behind

someone's back, I'm not interested in speaking with them. I have a

low tolerance for liars and exaggerators, fake and inconsistent people.

Why do people try so hard to fit in? Why can't they just be

themselves? I am drawn to those who are comfortable with who they

are and therefore accept others at their most honest states.

I knew deep down there must be something wrong with me

because no matter where I went, I was always alone. I was the one

distancing myself. I could not let anyone in because I was too picky. I

wanted to find the perfect friend.

This body, this perception, it has pulled me back in my life– I knew

I need to connect with others, and the honest truth is that I wanted to,

but everything inside me held me back: my nerves numbing my legs and watering my eyes so I can't even see clearly; my unreliable memory that proves I have nothing valuable to add to a conversation; even the fear of not knowing if I can pronounce a word correctly, or if I couldn't find another word to substitute it fast enough so no one noticed I avoided it.

All I wanted to have was a best friend to talk to: to meet up over tea and discuss the meaning of life and whatnot. At the very least, I wanted someone I could count on to come shopping with me or just go for a walk with. I am just so tired of being alone all the time.

It then occurred to me that I did have a best friend – Irvine. But this was a tactic I had used since high school to avoid the truth: I would get a boyfriend; not just a boyfriend, but a best friend. Someone who would walk around town with me for hours just talking; someone who would be happy to see me and could pick me out of a crowd; someone who I could call up at any time and they would be there for me. Irvine has proven to be my favourite person in the world. I was undeniably in love with him, and he was my best

friend too. The only thing that bothered me was that he had other

friends, and I didn't. He would leave on a Saturday night and it would

baffle me that he could spend over six hours with his friends and leave

me behind, alone, just waiting for him. I was sick of it, but I had no

one else – I had nowhere to go. I knew the only solution was for me to

have my own friends, and that I could never expect Irvine to put his

whole attention on me… but I was hopelessly awkward and alienated.

I knew he didn't deserve to carry my whole weight on his shoulders –

I needed the support of someone else.

I laid on my bed, covered myself with the only blanket I had and

my scarf, in an attempt to keep warm. I could feel I was getting a cold

and I lightly closed my eyes.

I later woke up at three in the morning. My stomach ached,

reminding me that I had had only a few teaspoons of oatmeal the day

before. I couldn't fall back asleep because my mind started racing with negativity: *Why am I here. I'm not flexible, I can't even touch my toes. I'm not strong enough for this – I'm not physically ready for four hours of yoga every day. I don't have enough experience in yoga – I just started September last year. I will never teach yoga when I get back home: I'm too shy. Why did I waste my money for this? I should have taken Irvine to the Philippines. Then we would be warm, instead of being here in this fucking freezing place. I need to buy a sweater, but I don't want to go shopping alone.*

I went to school early to have a masala chai and a banana. Our second hour of Vinyasa class felt like it was directed at me. It was composed of different types of forward folds – my least favourite pose because I'm hopelessly stiff in my hamstrings. Our teacher told us not to bend our knees because we will not see progression if we do not push ourselves. I wanted to cry. Every pose we did I felt like rolling my eyes in anger. He had made this into an embarrassing and uncomfortable class for me. I felt picked on, and I knew it wasn't on purpose, but he had sequenced every pose that I could not do.

To find comfort, I told myself I could look for flights once there was Wi-Fi again – I allowed myself to consider giving up halfway and going to Vietnam earlier than expected. I mean, really, I could go anywhere – I could go home if I wanted to. I was so frustrated that I didn't care about the money, I would pay my debt once I got back home. I was done. I had come here to find happiness, and some sort of belonging and purpose, but here I was freezing for 20 hours of the day and sitting alone... I wanted to give up.

After class I went to my room to decide if I would even go back to continue the course. I walked onto the porch and looked around to see if I was being watched. A pigeon caught my eye because it was laying on its back, dead, right under my window. I held my breath and quickly closed the door. I closed the window and the curtains too.

I turned around and nervously laughed to myself. *What is happening to me today?*

After pacing back and forth in my room wondering what I should do, I went down to the front desk of the hotel to see if there was anyone there. A woman smiled at me from behind the counter.

"Hi, um, there's a dead pigeon on my porch." as I spoke, a woman from my class walked in and then laughed.

"That's too good." she said without missing a step. I smiled at her. I understood that she laughed at the ridiculous situation that I just happened to be in, which made it less of a "targeted" coincidence, but I was still on the edge of tears.

The woman behind the desk asked for me to explain again.

"There's a pigeon that died on my porch." I said slowly, trying to project a humorous perspective, as if I also thought this was too good to be true.

She told me that someone will get it sometime today. I said thank

you and went back to my room. I decided that I shouldn't stay in my

room too long because I didn't want to be there when they took the

pigeon. So, I ended up going to class.

In Pranayama (control of the breath), I found that I couldn't

breathe properly through my nostrils: I knew I was sick. My nose was

runny for the entire hour of pretending to breathe with everyone else.

I quickly became exhausted at the thought that I was now sick.

I stayed for Philosophy class, but I could barely keep my eyes open.

My body was weakening, and I missed my warm bed back home.

Our teacher explained that nothing is real unless you experience it

for yourself. At first, I did not understand because we learn so many

facts in school without experiencing it, and we have to trust that those

facts are real. Some students spoke out and started debating with him.

I took this time to look inwards and searched for an example for myself to understand: a childhood friend of mine has just given birth to a baby boy, but it wasn't real to me because I hadn't seen her during her pregnancy or held the baby afterwards: I hadn't experienced it for myself. In my head, she was still the young girl I knew in high school so many years ago. I knew her life had changed, and she was older now, but it wasn't real to me because I haven't seen her since then. I could not reflect, feel, and understand the change in her life because it was so distant to mine. I had put her on pause to live my new life in a new province.

Needless to say, it was very difficult for our teacher to express this statement, and the students didn't show any compassion. I became angry, because I was able to accept this statement, but others couldn't wrap their heads around the concept. I had accepted this statement, but it wasn't *real* to me until I practiced it and made the judgement for myself.

After anatomy, I didn't go to lunch – instead I went to the store and bought a jar of Nutella and conveniently they sold single spoons. I went to my cold, dark room and laid in bed eating Nutella from the jar with my new spoon. I tried cheering myself up with comedic videos, but I could feel this weight on my shoulders and in my heart. I looked at myself in the mirror and asked: "What are we doing here?"

Looking into my worn-down eyes, I broke down into tears, biting my lip and shaking my head trying to fight this weakness. My heart hurt. This feeling of loneliness wasn't a new experience, but rather something that I could not shake.

"No matter where I go, I will never be happy. Why can't I just be happy?" I sobbed, trying to stay quiet in case my neighboring classmates were in their rooms.

I sat in my sorrow until I had no more energy left. Then I forced myself to get ready for class and tried to forget the past two hours of self-pity.

During our Meditation class that night, I focused my energy on my third eye. It felt like it was releasing a light throughout my body, like someone held a glowing rod on my forehead between my eyes and it entered my body until I became illuminated from inside out. I had never felt anything like this in my life and it shocked me. I quickly disconnected myself from my meditative state, because I could feel my eyes water and the skin around them turn red. I wiped my eyes quietly, hoping no one else peeked around the room. It had made me so emotional, like I was so filled with contentment I started to cry. I wasn't happy – I wasn't anything in particular – more like I was just fully connected to myself for the first time in my life. Entirely connected to my energy, to this moment, and to my worldly body.

I sat on my butt with my knees curled up to my chest, and I rested my forehead on my arms which were folded over my knees. I tried to focus on my breathing. I needed to calm myself down before the class was over and dinner was served so that no one could see my red, dreary eyes.

As I walked by the steps of the school, heading in to have dinner with everyone else, I suddenly decided not to go in and kept walking. The man with the curly long hair sat in the lobby, and I felt myself reach out to him, almost as a cry for help. Physically, I did not move my arms, but my energy went sideways towards him. I was taken aback as my mind did not control this connection, and out of shock I kept walking to my hotel and didn't look back.

In my room, I messaged Irvine before going to lay down: "Kind of want to come home… What's wrong with me? Why can't I be happy?"

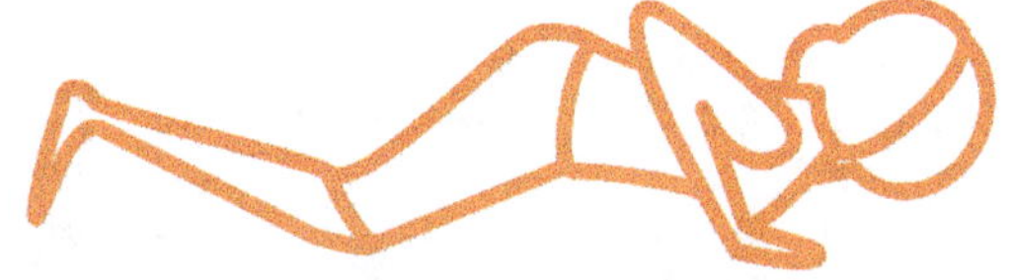

Chapter Four

Today was Diwali. We didn't have any classes because it was a holiday for the locals. I didn't go to the school for breakfast or lunch – I waited as long as I could and then went out to a café across the bridge. It was called Café de Goa, and not a lot of people went there – there would usually be a couple or a small group of friends sitting on the other side of the balcony, but I would always have a spot for myself overlooking the calming river and the chaotic bridge. I liked it here. I could watch the disorder on the bridge and the soothing waters below. I never asked for the Wi-Fi password because I was there to enjoy the present.

I felt beautiful today: I had a yellow scarf over my shoulders and chest, a shirt that my mom had given me from her travels in Asia, and pink pants which I had bought for pajamas a few days ago. I ate an eggplant curry while watching the tourists on the bridge struggle to get around the bulls who were looking for food. Women would have something in their purses that the bulls could smell and consequently they would stick their head inside trying to grab anything with their tongues. If the woman pulled away but was stopped by the crowd, the bull would try to run into her with his horns. You could tell if they were tourists or locals by the way they dealt with the bull. Some people walked by very confidently, like they had walked past the same bulls every day for the past few years. While the tourists were weary and tried to feed them until the bulls got out of hand. Also, I saw some who would touch the bull while mumbling to themselves – I assumed to be praying. It was interesting to watch.

On my way back, after I passed the bridge – becoming part of the chaos for a few minutes – I took my time going back to the school. I wasn't in a rush to go back into that cold room and be alone again. I projected a desire to run into a classmate: anyone to invite me to join them anywhere. But no one appeared.

I returned to the hotel and in the lobby, there were two classmates getting henna done from the woman who worked in the hotel. I forgot my nerves for a moment and asked them if they knew what time dinner was. One of the girls, closer to my age, said it was at 7 PM, then asked what I would be doing until then?

"Well, I've done everything that I wanted to do, so I'm not sure! What are you doing?" the words just came out of my mouth without any thought.

She told me that a few girls will be meeting on the rooftop to sunbathe and hang out for a while, and I was welcome to join. I said I probably will. I smiled while walking up the stairs and waited in my room for a while. I organized the clothes in the metal wardrobe and waited about 40 minutes until I went up to the rooftop. I hadn't been up there yet since I arrived.

No one was there when I managed to open the door. I walked to the edge of the roof and looked out at the view for a few seconds, pretending that I meant to come up here, and then quickly ran down the stairs. I spent the next three hours alone in my room. I never heard any footsteps or voices heading up to the roof.

I did look outside briefly to check if the pigeon had been removed. Now there was a lone pigeon looking at me from the air conditioning machine as if asking where his lover had been taken away to.

I watched comedies until it was dinner time, and I tried to find some confidence again. I wore the same outfit I did at lunch time, attempting to act like I wasn't completely underdressed for the chill in the air. The school had made a special dinner for tonight – Kadai Paneer, my favourite dish. They had also made some fried potatoes and vegetable sides. I ate slowly, trying to be included into the conversations beside me, but I wasn't involved: so much so that the girl closest to me put her elbow on the table to rest her head facing the end of the table, which acted as a wall to exclude me. I just looked at

my food and quietly left once I was done. I didn't speak to anyone.

I took a few minutes and went up to the roof, where I watched

some of the fireworks. I wondered how many accidents happened

during these past few days – every day we heard fireworks leading up

to tonight. I wished I would be able to see New Year's Eve in the

Philippines, because that is supposed to be completely insane, and I

imagined that this was nothing in comparison.

I stood in the cold asking myself why I came here. I knew deep

down I had to be here, but I couldn't figure out why. Why did I put

myself through all of this?

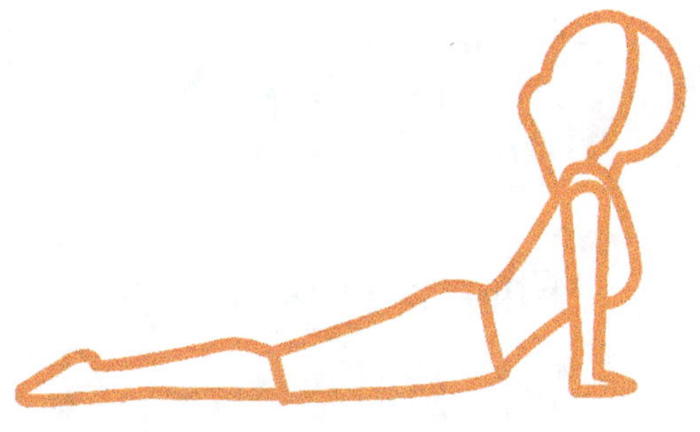

Chapter Five

"Let's get married." I sent Irvine a message as soon as I woke up.

"Okay baby." he replied.

"Let's have a family and build a house in the Philippines. I want to spend the rest of my life with you." I continued.

I was full of love this morning in Anatomy class. I felt so reassured that Irvine was the one and only true love of my life. My body cried to be pregnant, and I knew I wanted to experience parenthood with him. I wanted to wake up beside him every day and come home to him every night.

I also had the extreme urge to get high. This past week I've been wanting to escape my mind and I knew that being high would pull me away. I hadn't been high in over 6 years, but I knew it was the feeling

I craved. I just needed a break from these negative thoughts and sleeping wasn't an option anymore – now I had a busy schedule.

My sleep was getting worse the longer I stayed here too – I would toss and turn until 4 AM, and my alarm would go off at 5:30 AM. I knew my body could not handle it for much longer.

The German classmate came over to me in Hatha class and struck a conversation about the book I was reading – I had given up on looking *open for conversation* and decided to busy myself with my book before classes. We started talking about mental health issues and then depression was brought up. He said that as long as someone has a good support system – like family and friends – and a healthy lifestyle with exercise – like yoga – it will decrease the chances of that person getting depressed.

I thought "wouldn't that be nice". I have felt like I have been plagued with this depression and nothing I did would make it go away for the past couple of years.

The next morning was Sunday, and we woke up for our 4:30 AM jeep ride up the mountain to watch the sunrise. I was wearing most of the clothes I had brought with me to keep warm. I waited outside the school with some of the older students. One of my eyes kept tearing up from the gusts of wind through the narrow alleyway, and I could not control it. I just kept wiping my eye, knowingly taking a little bit of mascara off every time.

As a group, we started walking towards the bridge, and I quickly realized that I had never been on these streets before our mid-day break when all the shops were open, and the tourists flooded these narrow streets. This morning showed a more peaceful and vulnerable side of the town.

We passed the round-about that exploded my anxiety every time I walked through: this was one of the busiest areas where beggars, salesmen with postcards, and street-food vendors approached anyone who looked out of place. Today, it was completely deserted besides some baby cows searching for food on the ground. We started to walk across the bridge, somehow the half of the group that was behind me had disappeared momentarily and ahead of me there were just a handful of girls. I slowed down, watching them walk in pairs, analyzing my emotions to see how I reacted to the awareness of being alone in comparison. The wind was unbelievably strong, and I took out my camera to make a video I could later send to Irvine. My hair flew around as I shyly smiled for the video, hoping no one was behind me.

It was refreshing not to fight our way across the sea of tourists, motorcyclists, bulls, monkeys, and the odd painter to get to the other side of the bridge. We only passed a man who followed three donkeys carrying some materials. He was a smart man to make his journey this early in the day.

We walked up the steps and met the jeeps at the statue of the boy with an arrow. Seeing the statute again reminded me that I wanted to learn more about the Hindu religion. I was intrigued by all of the different Gods and Goddesses.

I got into the back of a jeep, facing inwards towards a girl from the 300-hour class. I envied the girls in the passenger seats which faced forward and looked out to where the jeep was headed. I knew I would have a difficult time with this ride, and wished it would be quick, before I felt the motion sickness.

This jeep reminded me of my trip through India in 2015, when we rode jeeps through the sands from Tordi Sagar to the road leading to Pushkar. I couldn't stop smiling on that ride because there were no seat belts in the back and I was tossed from my seat very frequently, sometimes even hitting my head on the roof. I had chosen to control

my emotions and take a positive perspective – ending up enjoying

that bumpy ride instead of succumbing to negative thoughts. I will

always remember that feeling.

We headed up a mountain in the dark, turning every 20 seconds or

so. I could not see more than three feet in front of the jeep, and I was

not able to anticipate when he was going to turn. I knew I was

nauseous when my legs went numb and I could feel my cheeks get

flushed. I needed some fresh air. I tried opening the sliding window

beside me twice unsuccessfully, trying to reassure myself between

attempts that I would be okay without it. My body was weak, and the

window required the persistence I did not embody.

The third attempt was much later, and I was more than desperate.

Centimeter by centimeter, I finally made it open, just enough to stuff

my fingers through the window to cool them down and then place on

my forehead, while simultaneously directing air onto my face. I tried to work up the courage to tell the driver to stop and let me out. I wanted to just walk back down the mountain. *Screw the sunrise.*

We turned so frequently there was not enough time in between to straighten my body upwards again. I knew I was going to puke. I grabbed a small plastic bag that I always kept in my bag to protect my camera in case it ever rained during my travels. I prepared myself to puke in front of the girl and two guys in the back seat with me, but suddenly we pulled up to a parking area. We passed other jeeps parked along the side of the road, then found a spot at the end of the road. We were pushed out of the jeep although I had wanted to lay down and fall asleep in the back seat.

We all collected at the edge of the mountain where a cement platform branched out in suggestion of where a store once stood. I looked around and saw a shop beside this platform. I peered in trying to see if they had some plain crackers I could nibble on until this nausea subsided. Before I could slip away from the group, everyone turned around and started walking across the street and up into a

covered walkway heading up the mountain. I walked with them for a

minute – tailing behind as I could feel the burn in my stomach creep

up. The irritation of the back of my throat was overwhelming and I

stopped at the second bench starting to cough and gag. I sat down

and I knew it was coming. I was so weak and feeling lightheaded.

Seemingly group after group started to arrive and walk past me,

looking at me clearly not being well. I decided to move away to

somewhere I could have some peace. I quickly walked back across the

street towards the platform where I saw a bench that appeared to have

been materialized just for me. I crashed down on the bench and

started gagging. Nothing came out the first few thrusts of my stomach

– there was nothing in me. My body did not give up. Pure stomach

acid came out and onto the ground beside the bench. It was thick and

slimy, and my spit fell long before I wiped my mouth with my

handkerchief. I took a drink of water and looked up to see the long-hair man from our school and the boy who sat beside me in the jeep.

They walked towards me, surprised to see me.

"Kaitlyn, what are you doing here?" I was surprised he knew my

name because I still didn't know his.

"I get motion sickness and that ride was rough! So... yeah I got sick."

I was feeling the adrenaline in my body.

He asked if I wanted to go up to see the sunrise because that's

where they were going, but I said no. I just wanted to lay down. I

didn't even want to go back down the mountain – I would rather just

stay here for a few hours and rest. He said he would stay with me

here. I tried to tell him not to, but he kept insisting. He told the boy to

get some masala chai, and we sat on the platform at the edge – he

dangled his feet and I sat cross-footed. It was quiet for the first few

minutes, while we looked out at the valley of mountains below us,

dusty and dark without the sunlight's touch. I turned to him and started asking questions to get him talking. I didn't want to say much, but I didn't want it to be awkward for him.

I asked where he was from and how did he start working for the school; did he do yoga and what kind of lunches were scheduled for the rest of the month. I asked him if the school would ever make naan because I loved naan bread. He said no since the kitchen doesn't have an oven to make it properly.

He started opening up: he told me how he struggled with being shy and quiet, and I related deeply.

"Growing up I always looked down. I could barely look someone in the eyes." he said.

He was now in a position where every day he had to push himself out of his comfort zone. I understood this. I had wanted a job where I would be pushed out of my comfort zone every day – and I knew I could do it because I was always an out-going person when I traveled.

I had applied to so many tour guide positions, and I had numerous

skype interviews, but no one saw the person I would have been had I

been in that position. It was difficult to promise them something they

could not see. And now I work behind a computer answering emails

and almost never picking up the phone.

I had brought my camera, but I did not have the nerve to take it

out and take pictures while he spoke. I faced him when he spoke, and

therefore my back was turned away from the sunrise. It didn't really

bother me that I had missed the sunrise. I had done this all before so

many times – the morning jeep ride or hike up the mountain to watch

the sunrise over the valley.

The fact that I was there on this day at the time had such a

powerful sense of belonging – like I knew I was supposed to be there.

I tried to believe that it was him who needed me to be sick and stay

behind for him to open up about his past; for me to be a listener and

not expect anything from this conversation. However, I now see that it impacted me in a way that made me reflect on my own life and specifically my career choice. I had faced so much rejection during secondary school and after graduation: all the beautiful dreams of becoming a better person were shot down because no one gave me a chance to blossom. I was starting down a doomed pathway. I needed this conversation to get myself back on track with my dreams.

The group later joined us, and we quickly separated from each other. I realized how it would have looked without any context of our conversation. I stood up with the girls who I would end up in a jeep with heading down the mountain. They encouraged me to take the front seat, which was nice because I could have the window open and let fresh air in and on my face. It was lighter out now and I could see the road and anticipate when we would turn. The road was bumpy, and my stomach was still unsteady, but going down was better than going up.

By the time we arrived back at the school, we had missed

lunchtime. I decided to go back to my room and take a nap – I had

this freedom because I had no friends to make promises to hang out

with.

I later woke up out of hunger. I rolled out of bed and decided a

pancake would be nice and light for me to test my stomach out. My

room was cold and so I dressed in my long black yoga pants, and my

grey sweater. As soon as I walked a few steps outside I knew it was too

much clothing. It was mid-day and the sun beat down on me harshly.

It took away my memory of the cold, windy night and made me take

it for granted, wishing it away behind the clouds. As I crossed the

bridge heading to Café de Goa, a mother stopped me, asking for a

selfie. I said sure because it seemed as if it was just her, but she quickly

called her family over and proceeded to take pictures of me with her

sons. I politely said thank you and walked away. I decided as I walked up the steps that I would eat and go back home – there's no point of sweating out here by myself.

At the café, I ate a lime and honey crepe and drank two glasses of masala chai. I took my time sitting there watching the odd white-water raft drift by while their passengers emptied into the river and then screamed to be pulled back up from the freezing water. I watched the visitors in the temple across the river, and how they walked around each level until making it to the top where their children would ring a bell. I didn't feel lonely today, but I felt like the day had passed me already and I would go back to my room then quickly wake up tomorrow.

I broke a large bill at the café because the server was very nice to me and I took advantage of the opportunity. I decided to walk around on this side of the bridge because I had not yet been around here. I had so much anxiety just walking to the café from our school, I wasn't ever interested in pushing myself to go around further, but today was different. I walked around and I saw the family that had asked me for

photos. I smiled and quickly walked into a store. There, an older man

greeted me. He sold jewelry and small statutes. I looked around for a

bit before he came over to test his salesmanship. I wanted a small

statue of Ganesh: I had not walked into that store knowing that is

what I wanted, but something inside of me picked a small golden

statue of Ganesh with four arms sitting on a lotus petal.

The man said Ganesh was for good luck and removal of obstacles. I

bought it for 250 rupees. I didn't bargain because I had more than

enough money for the rest of my stay here. He wrapped the statue in

a newspaper, and I stuffed it inside my sweater pocket. I held it with

both hands while walking back to the school. It felt like the statue was

glowing in my hands, and I wanted that energy to flow into me. I held

onto the statue trying to stay logical and within reality, but now my

path cleared easily – the crowds moved to either side and I felt

guided. It was a familiar feeling; like how I felt earlier this trip walking on the rocky shoreline and finding my perfect boulder to sit on while

I waited for my classmates to meditate in the cave.

The bridge that was constantly stuffed with people, motorcycles,

bulls, and monkeys became scattered and felt empty. I didn't break

my stride to cross the bridge. Looking around at the still buildings,

knowingly contrasting them with the chaos their walls covered. Life

seemed to pause as I soaked the scenery in.

My breath became noticeably relaxed, straightening my back and

feeling empowered; I suddenly felt like I wanted to stay outside and

enjoy the day. Across the bridge, I walked around the roundabout

with a statue in the middle – I didn't look at the statue, as I looked

into the vendors' stalls for the first time since I've been here. I looked

at what I've walked past so many times before but never dared to lift

my eyes towards. I saw some colourful scarves and was reminded of

my promise to my mother: I needed to get her a rainbow of scarves

while I was here. I touched the fabric to know the quality of the scarves and something pulled my attention out into the crowded

street for a second. I caught eyes with a true-looking hippie, which cut

through my skin and hit my deepest awareness. I quickly looked back

at the scarves, afraid of the feeling I just had. I brushed it off and

started contemplating if I should buy all the scarves from one place or

go around to various stores.

"This would fit my nephew." I could hear her smiling as she said

these words. I turned around to see her back towards me as she

grabbed a small vest from the wall. I had felt her presence walk

behind me and into the store. I smiled slightly, trying to channel a

"hippie vibe", but I was in envy of her. She wore her hair in

dreadlocks that fell over her breasts and crawled down her back. She

was in simple, brown, high-waist pants that flared at the bottom, and

a small vest that covered her shoulders but showed a carved stomach.

She was gorgeous.

I left the store because I could feel my jealousy kick in. I tried to think of what I could do today instead of going back into my dark room and sitting alone in the cold.

Down the road a bit, I got to an area where a few jeeps would park, gather their clients, and drive through the narrow streets. I started crossing the street to avoid the commotion and then I saw her pass in front of me. She was smiling as she passed me, almost in slow-motion with a beam of light behind her. She felt like a summer afternoon in my childhood. I felt a connection when we locked eyes. I walked behind her as we passed the jeeps, then she slowed down and turned to face me.

"Would you like to sit down and talk with me for a while?" she asked me with a smile. Her skin glowed with her natural appearance.

"Sure." the word came out of my mouth before I even registered her question. I reassured myself that we would be in a public area.

We continued down the road in a single file because a few jeeps were making their way into the commotion. I could tell from her facial features that she could be from the Middle East.

She turned and asked me where I was from.

"Canada." I didn't engage in a follow up question because I thought following her up this road was a proper time for silence, but she continued:

"Oh, so you're a native English speaker?"

"Yeah." I laughed because I do not think I have ever been asked that before.

"Do you want to sit by the river?"

"Sure." I smiled in politeness: I was fine with anywhere.

I could feel my guard was up while she continued to ask me questions as we climbed onto a rocky cliff on the side of the river. There were steps on either side, but she insisted that the rocks were more suited for us. I sat beside her, on the edge of the jagged rocks. On my left was nothing, just an eight-foot drop lined with layers of horizontal rocks all unevenly chipped and sharpened by the rising tide of the Ganga River.

I had a feeling that people could see us and were watching us. I tried to imagine what it looked like: I was completely out of place with my western clothes on.

She looked at me and said that I had a deep connection with nature. I thought of my childhood running around barefooted in the backyard and climbing the trees. I smiled, and calmly said "yeah."

I looked out to the river and found peace.

"And you have these dreams or visions that become real." I looked at her and cautiously said "yes."

She also said she could see that I had a good skill of detecting bullshit in others and I hated a liar – which I believed to be true of myself.

I didn't really engage with her, I only nodded and allowed her to say whatever she needed to say.

She then proceeded to tell me she was sorry that I have had to suffer so much in my life already. She said that I've faced a great deal of depression and loneliness throughout my life.

"It's unfair that you've been through all of that, you didn't deserve it, but you are so strong now. You have survived and overcome all that negativity, and now you're trying to give it meaning. What was the purpose of going through all of what you went through, if not to make something beautiful out of your life? Let me ask you this question, why are you here? Why did you come to Rishikesh?"

"I came here to find some happiness." I smiled when I saw her face light up. I knew it confirmed everything she was saying.

She had the comfort of no one I've ever met before – it was as though I was sitting there on that edge talking to myself. I looked at her, studying her face, it was like she was myself but from another life path. It was as if I had ran away from home and lived a nomadic life in India, just chasing happiness like I have dreamt about – she is exactly who I wanted to be.

She began to tell me about her life in the Himalayan mountains: working for a company rolling buds and performing ceremonies to get high with holy marijuana. She told me about her gurus and my interest peaked. I have always wanted to be so secluded and away from the chaos of the world, and just learn at the feet of a guru. I was also intrigued by the daily use of substance in pursuit of happiness

and enlightenment. She smiled and began to tell me about a

conversation with her guru.

"I told my Guru, I said: 'Papaji, I think I want to go to Rishikesh.'

'Miriam, you *think* you want to go. You should not follow your mind.

Your mind wants to go somewhere, but once you get there, it'll want

to go another place. And so on. You will never be content if you

always follow your mind.'" She said mimicking an Indian accent.

In that moment I let my guard down to enjoy the story. I smiled

while soaking up the way she spoke. She smiled at me, locking eyes as

if she could see through this vessel into my soul.

"Then I said, 'papaji –"

She did not finish her sentence as I fell backwards, completely

blacking out.

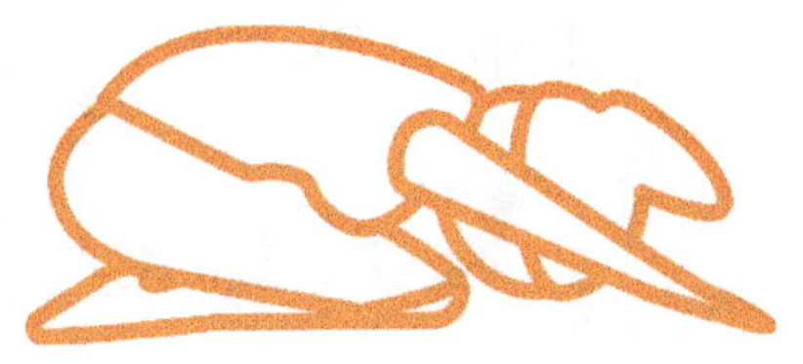

Chapter Six

I became aware of the blackness for a couple of seconds, and then I saw her – a blue goddess sitting crossed legged with long dreadlocks and holding the "om" symbol in her palm. Her body became blurred, as I quickly zoomed to her face. I knew deep down she was me all dressed up – it felt like looking into a mirror. I gave myself the smallest smile – a Mona Lisa smirk. Then I vanished, seeing only darkness, but fully aware that my lower lip was being sucked into someone's mouth. Shocked, I opened my eyes to see who it was, half-expecting to be back in my bed in my staff accommodation in Banff. I found myself bent backwards over a rock with Miriam trying to hold me by my right hand. I knew deep inside that kiss was a vision into the future. I quickly pulled myself back up and looked down at where I would have fallen. The thin layers of rock unevenly showing would have cracked my head open and pushed me into the river, had she not caught me.

I instantly felt like throwing up.

"I'm sorry, that's never happened before." I apologized for being human.

"Can I go to the water?" I asked. I wanted Irvine. I didn't even think I could move my legs; I was so weak.

She helped me down to the water, making me sit on third step up. She then asked:

"Is it okay if I wash your face?"

I swallowed nothingness into my dry throat, trying to forget the urge to throw up. I nodded my head and looked across the river while she washed her hands in the water. I saw a group of tourists who were practicing balancing yoga on the sandy part of the shore. I thought about how amazing this place is.

I noticed how dirty her hands were when she lightly held them over my face. Her nails were black underneath, and her palm was brown from dirt. She lightly rubbed my face, disregarding my mascara. Before sitting down beside me, she went down the steps three times to dip her hands in the glacier fed water then wet my face. She pulled my head to rest on her shoulder and asked if I was okay. I took a moment, then pulled my head back.

"I think I should go now." I just wanted to lay in bed and if I threw up again, at least I'd be in the privacy of my own room.

I could sense the sudden anger inside of her. She shook her head.

"I could feel you were so open before, but now after you fell, you have just closed back up".

"I'm just not feeling well." I said.

"Maybe you need to eat something… do you mind if I take you somewhere to eat?" she continued to argue why it would be good to stay with her, especially after I fell. She then explained how I fell, and she just managed to grab my arm in a split second and if she hadn't, I would have fell all the way down.

"I held you for two minutes, and I don't know how. It felt like I was given the strength to hold you in that moment, to protect you."

As we walked up the steps back to the main street, I could feel my body was sore. My left shoulder and my right buttocks were tender. I wondered what I looked like – my left shoulder had a mud stain, my makeup was partially washed off, and I was walking beside a true dirty hippie. I doubt anyone had seen me fall backwards, because no one came to help us or to see if I was alright.

We started walking away from my school neighbourhood, and towards a pathway where less stores or buildings were. I hadn't ventured out this far – it almost seemed like farmland, even though

the ground was hard and dusty. We just kept walking. She kept

talking, saying how pure and innocent my soul is. She said she has

never met someone so accepting and relaxed.

"Can I tell you something? I have been spending a lot of time alone in

the mountains, and so when I came back to Rishikesh I was a little

depressed. This morning, I asked the universe to meet someone to

spend some time with. And then when I walked by you today, it was

like your energy had reached out and tapped me on the shoulder. I

knew I had to speak with you… and you were in a store that had a

vest that would fit my nephew. I haven't seen him in so long. I am

going back to Israel in a couple of days actually."

She continued to dwell in the chances of meeting me, and how

comfortable she felt around me: as if we had known each other for all

of our lives.

We finally reached a nearby town after a long stretch of farming houses.

"I haven't been here in five years! I used to live here. Just around the corner. Do you mind if I check it out?"

We passed a few restaurants along the way, and I yearned for just a sip of water. Although I felt comfortable with her, I knew I needed to embrace every moment and just let her take me where I didn't know I needed to be. We turned down a small road and then turned right into a courtyard. She spoke to the owner of the hotel who brought us up to see his wife. I just smiled and watched the joy on Miriam's face. It felt like she had needed this walk-through memory lane, before returning home to Israel.

I stood there awkwardly until a couple came up behind me and I had to move out of the way. Miriam widened her eyes and became very excited to see the couple who had passed me. They knew each other. They took us to their room, where I waited in the doorway. She

asked if he had a guitar she could borrow, and that we would only go

to the roof for a bit.

We took the stairs up to the rooftop, which was just a small area,

enough for six people to lay down side by side. She sat down and

worked on the guitar. I tried to pay her no attention, so she didn't feel

rushed. The daylight faded through the forestry hills, kissing the

buildings here and there. The sun was already behind us, heading

down for sunset within the next couple of hours. The sky was a

smoky pink mixed with orange, and black birds flew around in their

groups. The contrast of the birds in the sky looked like a painting

resurrected. From here, the buildings that hung on the side of the hill

across the river looked warm and inviting. The overstimulation of

crowds, noise, and no order was all lost in the romantic lighting. I

desired to jump up and fly across to overlook the commanding environment that tormented me with fear and anxiety – seeing it below my flying feet as harmless as I knew it logically was.

The guitar had sung me back to the moment and she explained this song was written for her last lover, but she broke her heart. She said it did not matter, because her feelings are the same for me now. My stomach dropped – I had forgotten about the vision I had. *Would it be her?*

Regardless, I tried to enjoy every second. She played a beautiful song, while I sat with my eyes lightly closed and meditated. This beautiful scene was ended by the guy who gave Miriam the guitar. He had to take it back.

I had no sense of time at this point. The sunset seemed to stay permanently while she got closer to me. First touching my knee, and then moving my hair. I could smell her body odor, and her unwashed dreadlocks.

She pulled out some dried Tobacco and rolled a cigarette for herself. She asked me if I smoked, and I simply said no. I didn't explain that I hadn't smoked since my trip to Indonesia with my brother last year. I did not tell her I was almost one year sober as well. It wasn't important enough.

The smell of this cigarette reminded me of an old boyfriend of mine: that one day, where we were laying on the couch in his basement, chain smoking between long sessions of making out. That sense of safety and love filled my body with every inhale. I smiled to myself, remembering the good times.

She moved closer and slowly kissed my cheek. I tried not to look at her. She kept telling me how beautiful I was, and how I should be treated like a princess.

"What's wrong? You don't look as bright anymore? It looks like something is troubling you."

"I'm just thinking about my boyfriend at home." As I said these words, I quickly thought of Irvine.

"Of course," she took a long drag from her cigarette and then put it out on the ground behind her, saving half of it for later.

"I was once like you. I had a girlfriend back home, but I fell in love with someone on my travels. She taught me that we can love multiple people. I still loved my girlfriend back home, but I was able to explore this new love with this new girl just for that day. We live in these societal binds that make us think that polygamy is a bad thing. But you need to break out of those rules. You need to love who you love at any moment. You know my father and my mother are not together: they were just friends. But they knew they had to come together to make me."

She went on about how marriage is just a piece of paper, and we were never meant to be tied to one person for the rest of our lives.

Finally, we sat in silence. I looked down at her hand on my knee

and saw that she had the exact tattoo I was going to get back in 2015.

"I wanted this exact tattoo in that exact spot like three years ago when

I was in Goa." I said with excitement.

"You were in India three years ago?" she asked with a serious tone.

"Yeah, but only for two weeks." I replied innocently.

"I came here three years ago to get this tattoo. I met my friend in

Delhi and she wrote this in her own handwriting. I love the way she

made it her own. I feel her energy is with me through her art piece.

Can you touch it?"

"Touch your tattoo?" I awkwardly asked.

"Yeah. I want to feel your energy." She grabbed my hand lightly and

placed it on her other hand. She looked deeply into my eyes, although

I looked down at her tattoo wondering what the odds were.

She then leaned over and started to kiss my lips and there it was: she sucked my lower lip into her mouth but only deep enough just to feel her lips. This was the exact feeling from my vision earlier. I pulled away and then looked around us: there were men working on a rooftop beside us, putting bricks on top of each other to make a wall. On another rooftop there was a couple hanging their laundry on the ropes tied to two poles. I wondered what we looked like. I was dressed completely in western clothing that I had bought with my credit card because I never have enough in my bank account and sitting beside me was a woman made from the donations and guidance of others.

"Do you mind if we eat something?" I asked, playing the weak and sick card. This situation was getting uncomfortable for me, and I didn't want to taste her last cigarette anymore, even if it reminded me of some high school days.

We started going down the stairs when she saw the couple on the rooftop hanging clothes and asked them if they knew a good place to eat – somewhere with good naan. She then realized she knew the girl and they reminisced of their time living here. She said they just got back yesterday after two years living in Australia.

The couple had told us about a good restaurant nearby, and so we went out to search for it. I didn't catch the name of the restaurant but thankfully she did. As we walked around, she asked strangers where the restaurant was. It was useful that she knew some Hindi. I saw how her confidence grew every time she spoke with someone in front of me. It made me miss speaking Filipino in the Philippines.

We finally found it – it was a part of a hotel. We walked to the edge of the hotel and saw a couple sitting at a table under a tree. She walked up and spoke with the couple, asking where the restaurant was. The staff quickly saw us and pulled a table from storage, setting two chairs beside it. I washed my hands at the outdoor sink and watched her flourish in her conversation. I was not envious, because I knew I could do that – I *have* done that – but it was just interesting and somehow fulfilling to watch her. She mentioned her name, and I remembered it this time: Miriam.

She finally sat down with me, and we both looked for naan on the menu, as I had told her earlier that I've been searching for some proper naan, but there wasn't any. She stood up and said thank you to the staff, but we are looking for naan. I followed her out of the hotel compound, feeling a little embarrassed. *I would have never done that.*

We walked back towards where we entered this small town, where she spotted a local's restaurant. As we walked in, she spoke with the owner and asked how his naan bread was. He smiled and wobbled his head side to side while holding up his right hand with this index and thumb together forming a circle. She smiled at me as we sat down.

"Every time I look at you, it makes me smile." I could see her admiration through her hazel eyes. Her eyes were familiar: like my mothers. It was a brown and green mixture that animated in the perfect lighting.

I couldn't continue to look back at her, I just smiled and looked down at the menu. She ordered two curries, rice, and naan bread. She smoked the rest of her cigarette that she had from the rooftop. The fans on the walls reminded me of a restaurant Karen had brought me to in Manila's China Town.

I forced myself to eat as much as I could, but we did not finish the large servings. I had enough money in my pocket, that was cushioning the Ganesh statue, to pay for this meal but she said: "Wait outside, I'll be right there."

I stood on the edge of a closed store nearby and watched the odd car drive by. She spoke to the owner for a while, so I stretched my legs on the edge of the steps. I lifted the palm of my foot onto the step, keeping my heel down on the road, then pressed my body forward until I felt the stretch in the back of my legs. I took in deep inhales, enjoying the stretch.

When she finally joined me, her mood had changed. She looked angry and frustrated, but I didn't ask why. On our way back, I noticed how the street had completely transformed: the stores had their lights on, and the streets were even more crowded than usual. I hadn't realized until now that I haven't been out after our free time from 2-5PM. If I didn't eat dinner at the school, I didn't eat at all.

She started talking about Tantra – a new "part" of yoga that focuses on the passionate sensual experience with someone else, either through physical contact or sex. I instantly felt uncomfortable because I knew Irvine was the one that I wanted for the rest of my life and I did not want to mess that up. I never want to hurt him – especially after his ex-wife cheated on him. I tried to explain that I've hurt my boyfriend before, and I promised never to hurt him again.

"I love you, and I know you love me too. I saw you open up to me today. I see your soul. I see you. How beautiful you are. We met today for a reason. It is our destiny to be together." she said as we stood in the alleyway of my school.

I had nothing to counter what she said, because I knew we did meet for a reason, but this was not it.

"Just let me come to the rooftop at least. I just want to spend more time with you. Please. It was meant to be, can't you feel it?"

I shifted my weight: a clear sign I was uncomfortable. I could see some of my classmates on their porches smoking and listening to music, while others tried to pull them back inside to dance. I knew my experience here was completely different. My experience anywhere has always been different to those around me.

"You need to choose to leave the way the western world lives; you can love me tonight and still love your boyfriend back at home. It's just in your mind."

"No... I really should go now. I'm sorry."

"Can we just spend a little bit more time together? We can go somewhere else?" she confidently waved her right hand around as if she had somewhere already planned.

I hesitated. I did not want to stay out. I felt gross and tired – I just wanted to shower and sleep. I pointed to the alley between my hotel and the next, and we walked over. I didn't want anybody to see us: her fighting to spend the night with me, and my useless silence.

She hugged me once we got into the alley. I reluctantly hugged her back, keeping my hips back. I pushed her away and held her hands. I looked at her, but I didn't see her.

"I'm sorry." and I walked away, almost running up the stairs into the lobby and then fully running up to my room. I made sure not to turn on the lights in case she was waiting below to see which room was mine.

I instantly checked my phone, to see if the WIFI had come back on – it hadn't. I sent Irvine a bunch of messages, telling him I'm home though it probably wouldn't send until morning. I was embarrassed to tell him I fainted and saw myself as a Goddess. As I sat in darkness, I realized I did not know who the Goddess was. I wanted to make sense of my vision and finding out if that Goddess meant something might make it clear.

My sweater smelt like her armpits. I took it off, but I had nothing warm to wear to sleep, so I put it back on and tried not to let the smell bother me. I laid down shivering, trying to think if today was reality or just a dream.

Chapter Seven

Yesterday I must have twisted my body when I fell unconsciously forward onto the wet ground, then bounced backwards into the position that I woke in with Miriam holding my hand. My body was sore, and the sweater had a large mud stain on my left shoulder, so I went to class without it.

It was cold, and I only had an undershirt on. I counted the steps as I walked up to the classroom – 60. 60 steps before I just didn't care anymore, and I was out of breath. I crawled into the classroom and laid down my mat. I held my knees to my body and wrapped my big scarf around myself. The wind was loud this morning, sending shivers down my spine. I could feel my whole body was sore, not from my fall, but it felt as though I was fighting a cold. I wasn't surprised by my own diagnosis – a lot of my classmates had fallen ill already.

Whenever we did an inversion during our two hours of Vinyasa flow, I could feel my sinuses expanding and filling up. After class I went to my room quickly and checked my body for any marks from when I was unconscious. My shoulders were fine, although the left was a little tender. I was surprised when I felt my glutes because a sharp pain came from my right buttocks. There was a deep cut that ran four inches on top of a bruise that rested as a blotchy circle. The cut was healing already and looked like it would scar my skin. I had a couple scars on my body that I thought represented a certain chapter in my life. Both were on my wrist – one from a day where my ex-boyfriend had challenged me to lift a washed-up tree trunk and despite the wood cutting through, I lifted it to show my strength. The irony was that my strength would prove to be useless against him later on in our relationship and leave me with more bruises and invisible scars. The second scar was not more than an inch over on the same wrist. It occurred when I was packing up my stuff from my staff accommodation in Banff, a metal shelving had caught my wrist

as to say *it'll never be the same.*

I felt deep down that this scar marked something, an end of one

chapter and ultimately the beginning of another, but I didn't have

enough awareness to understand what that last chapter was. What

was the meaning of my vision, and how would my life change now?

I laid in the back row of the classroom for our Pranayama class,

shifting my weight from my right buttocks. I was not able to breathe

properly through my nose due to a head cold. I later fell asleep in

Philosophy for a few minutes.

Between Simon's class and our Anatomy class, I just stood up and

looked out the window. I had no thoughts in my head, my body just

got up and walked to the window. I needed to look outside for a

moment and that's when I saw it: among some other things, there was

a painting on the porch below us. It was her. It was the Goddess I saw.

I couldn't believe my eyes. I tried to stay calm and grabbed my phone

to take a picture in case I didn't believe myself later. Then our

Anatomy teacher came in and I obediently sat back down. I looked at

the picture I took, and it wasn't very clear. I made a mental-note to

take another picture after this one-hour class.

After class, it wasn't there anymore; the painting of the Blue

Goddess that I had envisioned as myself was gone. I kept my cool

because I didn't know what this meant. I still did not know who the

Goddess was. I skipped lunch and went straight to my room, where

the WIFI had finally come back on. I started searching for "Blue

Goddess in Hindu Religion".

I expanded my search after a while, and just typed in "Hindu

Gods". I found her, but she wasn't a *she* – his name was Shiva. His

name meant the auspicious one.

I didn't know what this meant. I didn't see the connection between Shiva and I, or what he could have given me. I was so sure my smile in the vision was me giving myself permission to be happy – but how do I be happy?

I saved a photo and asked our Hatha teacher after class who that was. She confirmed that it was Shiva – the creator and destroyer. When our class finished, I went outside to put on my sandals, and I happened to look up at the moon. It was a crescent moon, like the one depicted in Shiva's hair. I stopped for a moment, trying to find a logical explanation. I told myself that crescent moons happen twice a month, there was a good chance of seeing it.

The next day during Philosophy Simon surprised me with a lesson revolving around the Hindu God Shiva. He confirmed most of what I had read last night. Simon had mentioned Shiva before, but my notes only read "Shiva – that which is not – Om – Universe song", I had no idea Shiva was a Hindu God. I was in awe and hung onto every word he said, trying to make some sense of why I would envision Shiva.

He continued into the eight limbs of Yoga: Yama (Social Disciplines), Niyama (Self-Discipline), Asanas (Body Postures), Pranayama (Control of the Breath), Pratyahara (Control of the Senses), Dharma (Concentration), Dhyana (Meditation), Samadhi (State of Realization).

I took some time during our break to look up more facts about Shiva. I learned that he was depicted with blue skin because he held poison in his throat to protect mankind. Shiva's hair contains the Ganga's flow to calm it down and let out a small stream so that the earth isn't overwhelmed with its power. His third eye represents how meditation and yoga has allowed Shiva to refine his energies and enhance his perception of the world around him. He is sometimes depicted with two faces – one female and one male.

There was so much information about him and what he represented, but none of it really resonated with me. I didn't know how to proceed.

I knew Miriam would be in town for the next two days, and therefore I stayed at the hotel during our breaks: I started going up to the rooftop to sunbathe. I saw a handful of students doing the same thing and I realized I hadn't been the only one without friends. I started working on our big project due at the end of the month while enjoying the sun. I worked up the courage to lay there with just my sports bra and my capris to get a better tan. I have never been comfortable in my own skin – growing up, I've been told that I was too fat or too skinny; that I had to build more muscle and get in better shape – but seeing everyone else feel comfortable no matter how amazing their body was or how aged, they did it so why couldn't I?

The sun was going to set around 4 PM, but at 3:30 PM I knew that a group of the 300-hour students would come up to the roof to practice, and I would make sure to be down in my room before that.

When I went onto my porch to read and I saw that the pigeon had found a new partner. They both looked at me while I pulled my chair out. I looked around and there were two ladies out on their porch – one beside me and the other down at the end of the hotel. I waved and smiled before I sat down to enjoy my book.

Chapter Eight

There was a storm last night, and therefore the Wi-Fi was still out when I woke up today for our Vinyasa class. I almost didn't want to go because of the rough sleep I had endured overnight. The morning seemed to be non-eventful as my body was on autopilot while my brain was completely blank. During our afternoon break, I went to get lunch at the Café de Goa, but I was stopped by three of my classmates at the door of our hotel. The German guy was there, and he asked if I wanted to join them for lunch. They were comparing restaurants and trying to decide where to go, as there was a girl in our class who had food poisoning and she hadn't been able to participate for four days already. I said that there was a place that I go often, and the food was fine.

They followed me across the bridge and up the steps. One girl, Caitlyn, spoke with me for the majority of the way. She didn't eat at the café but decided to get a smoothie at another coffee shop back across the bridge afterwards. I went with her, losing the other two along the way. We figured out we had the same birthday and we both grew up in Ontario. I felt at ease with her, and I began to tell her my experience with Miriam a couple of days ago.

"I think I sound crazy." I smiled, shaking my head, and rubbing my forehead with my right hand.

"No, you're in a holy city in India: this is where you're supposed to experience stuff like that." She reassured me that it wasn't a shameful experience.

I started to wish I had written down everything that happened from that day before I forgot. I had just been so taken aback these past couple of days I wasn't sure what I was supposed to do and why I experienced all of that. When I was back at my room, I started to write down bullet-points:

- Tattoo
- Vision
- Papaji
- Guitar
- Sunrise
- Sunset

I was too lazy to elaborate on anything because the Hatha class was beginning soon and I had to get ready.

I skipped our meditation class to sleep early, as I felt so exhausted after missing my usual rest time this afternoon.

In the morning, our second Vinyasa class was all about balance, and I thrived. I loved testing my body to balance on one foot with the other leg up in the air tangled in between my arms in *Bird of Paradise*. It was the first time I had ever tried this pose and despite my leg not being straight up into the air due to my hefty hamstrings, I succeeded pulling my whole body off the floor and onto the platform of one foot. My eyes glazed over, and I had the feeling I used to get when I performed my katas in front of my Sensei. This class felt like a dance:

a swift, never-ending movement that calmed my body and opened

my heart. I had forgotten that I had wanted to quit altogether not too

long ago.

The day went by slowly, as usual, and I sunbathed on the rooftop. I

approached one of the girls also tanning and asked her to join me on

a walk one of these days to take some photos for social media. I felt

like I was overcoming the dark depression I had arrived with.

Meditation became the highlight of the day. As a class, we were

sitting in a circle, but I was behind everyone with my back on the wall

for extra support: we sat on the ground all day and by the time for

meditation, my body was weak. I closed my eyes and listened to our

teacher lead us down a mental pathway into a meditative state. It felt

like my eyes closed a hundred times without ever moving my eye lids.

I focused my energy throughout my whole body, starting from the

top of my head down towards my legs. I didn't know what I was trying to do, but my whole body awakened. I could feel the energy of being alive throughout my whole body. I became aware of every muscle, every bone in my body, all alive with this radiant energy. It felt like I was being hugged from behind, but I knew that was impossible because there was a wall two inches from my back. I could feel the touch of someone's warmth on my back and over my arms, it reminded me of a time when Irvine had come behind me and embraced me while I did the dishes. I felt an enormous amount of love and warmth radiating from my heart. I felt so loved and appreciated by myself. I felt like a sunrise. *Did I just hug myself?*

I focused my energy back towards my throat and then into my third eye. It was surreal. I felt the thumb of someone else pressed deeply into my forehead between my eyes. I opened my eyes to see who was there, but no one had moved. I rubbed my forehead to check if there was something there, but there was nothing. I quickly closed my eyes and regained focus – I didn't want to lose this feeling. But it had left. My body was warm and weak. My fingertips, which had been almost blue and numbed with coldness, were now plump with blood and burning red. I had increased my blood flow around my body without moving. My heart rate was at a resting rhythm, but my body felt exhausted.

The next night I was invited out for dinner with two girls from our class, and they brought me to a café on the second level. There was music playing loudly, and it felt like a bar, but we were in a holy city where no alcohol could be sold. We spoke about opening Chakras, but I wasn't familiar with what a Chakra was. They explained to me that there were certain areas from your head to the end of your spine that contained locked energy, and through meditation people can unlock theirs. It was all too fanatical for me, although it reminded me slightly of my meditation last night, I didn't think too much of it. We started talking about social anxiety and I saw we had more in common than I expected.

They also asked about my love life. They were both single, but I

had a boyfriend back at home to talk about. My heart grew warm, and

I could feel how much I missed him. I smiled when I spoke about how

we met and how both of our previous relationships were painful and

discouraging, but out of the ashes we saw a beautiful chance to

relearn how to love and trust again.

The next three days I was almost never alone. I went out for hot

chocolate with a girl in my class every day after Vinyasa, and during

the break I was on the rooftop doing my assignment surrounded by

other students. I was gaining flexibility in our classes as well: I could

stand on a wooden block with my left foot folded in Half Lotus pose

and forward bend to touch the ground in front of the block, keeping

my right leg straight. But unfortunately, this was only after lunch, so I

was still feeling a little unworthy during the morning classes.

On Thursday, I went by myself for hot chocolate, and I sat on some

steps to look out onto the river. It was cold and windy. Thursdays we had another schedule, with just the physical classes and the rest of the

day free. I sat by the river until my hot chocolate was cold. I took in

the moment, watching the river slowly move by. I wasn't sad or

angry, but I wasn't happy either: I was just taking in the view and

trying to capture the moment so I could remember this in the future.

These steps were near where I sat with Miriam that day, and although

I didn't consciously think about it, I knew this area of the river had

put its mark on me.

Looking out over the flowing water, which hummed louder now

with no one nearby, I thought of going home, and how this month

was almost over. I felt like I did not achieve anything or explore as

much as I had anticipated. I let my mind control me and stop me

from experiencing more. As I got up to leave, I looked around and

saw a café that I would later go to for lunch.

Working on my assignment in my room proved to be challenging

with so many distractions nearby. I decided to go for an early lunch, as my breakfast was just a banana and a hot chocolate. I walked

through the windy roads and found that café I had spotted earlier. I

walked up from the steps and tried to figure out the layout of the

restaurant – there was definitely an upstairs seating area, but I didn't

know if I could just walk up there or I needed to have someone to

greet me first. I ended up sitting on a plastic chair on the first floor

and waited for someone to come welcome me with a menu. I sat there

for five minutes reading the book I had brought. I moved the chair

beside me to make some noise, and I made eye contact with someone

in the kitchen who then called for someone. A guy came out with an

interesting eye set and gave me a menu. He must have had a glass eye,

as I couldn't tell if he was looking at me directly. He stood there for a

couple of minutes while I quickly looked through the menu. I looked

at him and smiled, as if saying "I don't know yet." and he went to the

back.

On the menu there was a grilled cheese sandwich with black olives and tomatoes. I didn't know whether the cheese would be vegan or organic, but I thought either way I can't go wrong. I gave him my order after he brought me some masala chai. I continued to read my book, glancing at the river every now and then. Only when the food came, did I start to think about that day with Miriam, and wondered if it was all just a dream. I thought what the odds are that it truly happened. Why would it have been Shiva I saw as me, and what does that mean for me now? What was I supposed to do?

I looked in front of me at the wall covered with a stained cloth and realized it was Shiva looking directly at me. I shook my head in disbelief. I smiled and, in my head, I asked the painting: *"what am I supposed to do now?"*

I looked into his painted eyes, opening my heart for an answer that didn't come, or at least I couldn't recognize.

That night I ran into a girl who was just sitting in the lobby of the hotel waiting for something to do. I asked her to come for dinner with me and we went to the same café I went to the other night with the two girls. I had pizza while we talked about our boyfriends. I told her that I thought we would get engaged when I got back home. I explained how we both have asked each other multiple times to marry one another, but I wanted a *real* proposal.

I noticed I was starting to forget the day with Miriam and was trying to remember it as a dream. I wanted it to be something my mind made up. I didn't speak to anyone about it to keep it from feeling real.

Later, I hand washed my laundry, as I did every couple of days because I didn't have many clothes with me. I let the clothes soak while I organized my backpack. I laughed to myself thinking what if I left my money in my pocket, then realized I had. I ran into the washroom pulling up my black pants and grabbing the money carefully folded in the back pocket. I was half-crying half-laughing as I pulled them carefully apart and let them dry off on my face towel.

We had Wi-Fi back after another storm last night, and I was scrolling through random pictures while laying on my bed. I then saw my co-worker had gotten engaged. I was happy for her, but I thought about Irvine and I, and asked myself: *would we really get engaged when I got back home?* I didn't want to mimic someone else in the shadow of "well they did it, I want to too". I didn't want to think for the rest of my life that I got engaged right after my co-worker did. I felt a little jealous and I tried to focus on other things.

During Hatha, we were sitting waiting for our teacher to come into the room. As she finally came, she walked past me and touched my shoulder while crouching down. She asked, "Why until now you have been quiet?"

"There's nothing going on in my head so there's nothing to say." I tried to laugh to make it less humiliating. I could feel the glances from the other students who had overheard her question, but I focused on her face.

My whole life people have gone out of their way to tell me I'm too quiet, and I hate it. I am not shy, I just have nothing to say. I'm inside of my head, examining the people around me, trying to find the right people to surround myself with. I'm awkward because I don't know how to react, and that's why I've always let everyone else carry the conversation. Social settings make my anxiety kick in.

It's true what I said to her, I didn't have anything in my head that affected anyone other than myself. My thoughts did not need to be spoken. The spotlight definitely did not need to be on me because what I'd say would be quickly allocated as an unworthy topic. I've tried to say what's on my mind, but time and time again I got shot down.

I understand why most things happen and I can conclude a logical explanation, but I am not knowledgeable. I cannot list facts or names or remember dates, but I can remember particular feelings. Feelings from my past have been the stronghold on how I predict personalities, actions, and outcomes today. However, that doesn't make good conversation when meeting new people.

This normally doesn't bother me until I compare myself to my older brother who is more social, confident, intelligent and successful. Our parents always said he would do great things. They told him to strive for government jobs where he would change the world.

As the instructor walked to the front of the room to start class, I asked myself: *"Why me?" Why can't I be like my brother? Why am I cursed with this over-thinking, self-shaming, unmotivated mind?"*

The next morning, I woke up to messages from my brother, showing me pictures of his new downtown apartment. I was happy for him, but I thought about how Irvine and I were just barely making

it by. I felt like we would struggle for the rest of our lives, pay-check to

pay-check, and I did not want that. I just wanted to be comfortable. I

do not have high standards or rich taste, but I knew I would continue

to be unhappy if we couldn't even afford a decent place for our

children to grow up in.

Needless to say, I was feeling down today. Jealousy wasn't the word

I would use to describe how I felt, but rather I thought: *Why not me?*

Why can't I be given a chance? Why do I have to face an inner struggle

as well as an outside struggle?

I remembered all the jobs I applied for that didn't even give me an

interview. Fast food restaurants that I lowered my expectations of

myself to even apply to, never reached out with interest.

I thought about how I hadn't taken any photographs that I had

wanted to take while being here, just because I was scared to go out by myself with a camera. I was nervous to take pictures of the local shop owners, or tourists flooding the streets. I just wanted someone to walk with me. I just did not want to be alone anymore.

I saw myself feeling disappointed and angry, and I knew it wasn't supposed to be this way. I thought I had given myself happiness. I thought I was overcoming this depression that dominated the past two years of my life. I felt like I failed a test. I should have been able to accept the success of others without comparing them to my own journey. I should have been able to be happy for them and help them celebrate their milestones, but instead I sat in self-pity and accused the world of being against me.

I was crying to myself in a long, hot shower, when I realized that I needed to change my perspective. I knew deep down, although I have been filled with disappointment, that everything happened for a reason. I didn't get those part time jobs during school so that I could focus on my studies and graduate with honours – not to mention that

I was able to have the time every week for yoga classes which sparked my love for yoga. I didn't get those travel jobs that I applied to throughout Asia because I would have eventually broken up with Irvine, and I wouldn't have the greatest love of my life anymore. I also would not have had a job in Banff working behind Deb who inspired me to become a yoga instructor, and therefore I would not have booked this trip to India. I would not be here if I got what I wanted back in 2016.

I fell asleep later after watching comedies, trying to suck myself out of this reality for a bit.

On November 28th, I taught Vinyasa in the second hour. I had a flow that was unlike the others, and I thought it was easy to teach because I had been taught a similar class when I first started. I was taught that it was a moon salutation, but we learned already that the moon salutation was the same as the sun salutation but with a half-moon pose instead of just a step backwards into equestrian pose.

What I had learned was probably just a western invention. I was glad to be learning yoga in the Yoga Capital of the world because everything felt authentic.

The class I taught started off with my classmates on their backs resting on a body pillow, with their legs in butterfly. Reclining Butterfly – I loved this pose because it opens the chest and the hips. I calmly brought them through a meditation while they lay there. My warm-up was harder than I would have liked if I was the student, but where I started to fail was doing the flow itself. We did one side at a time and it was supposed to be quite simple, but no one seemed to understand what I was saying. I tried to keep calm, but I ended up forgetting which way they needed to go next. I wanted to give up halfway through the class. Thankfully, I had some help from one of the girls, and we got back on track.

The decompression was quick because they needed to be in a laying down position for 5 minutes at least, but I was cutting it close to the

45-minute time limit. I ended up going 7 minutes over the time, but I don't think they noticed really. I sat there while the teacher gave me critiques in front of everyone. It was obvious I messed up a couple of times, but he said he liked how I taught and all my alignment cues. I did get a few minor things wrong, and I was focusing on those. They exploded in my head. I became so embarrassed. I thought it was a disaster even though most of the students said it was well done. But I decided that I could not focus on this failure now: I still had to complete the assignment that was due tomorrow.

I sunbathed while I worked on the assignment, until I got too hot and uncomfortable. I then walked to the same café where I had sat with Shiva for lunch. I ordered the same grilled cheese sandwich and worked until 4:30 PM when I headed back to shower and dress warmer – preparing for the rapid temperature drop. From 4 PM until the next morning around 10 AM, I would be frozen besides the sweating during our Vinyasa classes that quickly cooled and left me

shivering within seconds of being in Shavasana.

I later handed the assignment in and took myself out to the German

café for a well-deserved pancake smeared with Nutella and topped

with fresh banana. I sat alone, enjoying my accomplishment.

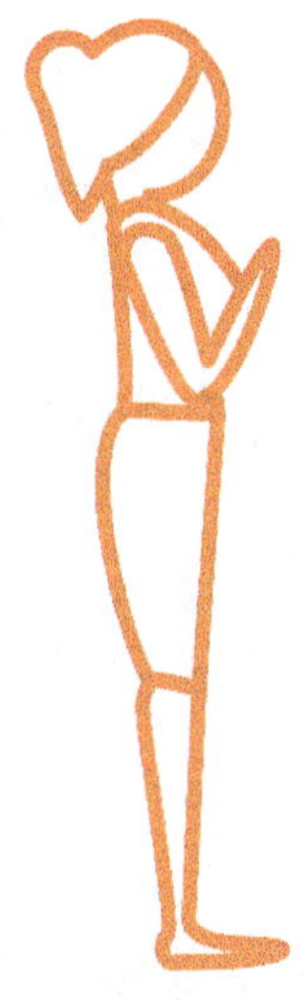

Chapter Nine

Saturday was our last Hatha class, and I would be teaching alongside our teacher because we had an uneven number of classmates. During the morning I brought my laundry in to be done for the first time this whole month: I was preparing for our graduation on Sunday, and then my flight to Vietnam the following day. I also received some henna on my left hand and right forearm. I had my hand covered in a flower and had her write on my inner forearm from my wrist to my elbow "you are not alone" translated into Hindu writing. I instantly fell in love with it and wanted to make it into a tattoo when I got home.

Around 3:30 PM Sarita messaged me asking what time we should meet up. I told her I can come back to the school for 4PM – as I was sitting with Shiva at the café by the river. She said 4:30 PM is fine, as the class starts at 5 PM. I got to the classroom at 4:26 PM and started to clear the space. I moved the pillows and blankets some people have left from our previous classes. I wanted this class to be special and different from what everyone else had prepared. I brought out 13 pillows and made a circle. I made the pillows close enough in the middle to allow their mats to be laid behind them, like rays of a sun. I realized I needed one more pillow for Sarita and adjusted my circle. I quickly became nervous waiting. *She should have been here by now.*

I placed blankets on the pillows, making sure everyone had one. I started looking at notes and thinking through what the class would look like. Sarita came in and she brought candles and incense. She told me to bring some wooden blocks into the middle of the circle and we can put the candles there for everyone to look at. We greeted everyone who came in, slowly adjusting to our setup.

Sarita whispered in my ear to rip some of my paper up so that everyone can write something on their paper to burn in the candles. I handed out a piece of paper to everyone and made sure everyone had a pen or pencil. We started the class by telling everyone to write something on the piece of paper that they want to let go after the growth everyone experienced this month. I knew right away I would have written "loneliness", but I was the teacher today. I thought maybe I can do a personal ceremony by the river tonight or maybe tomorrow where I can burn a letter or something on the Ganga.

One by one everyone burned their paper. Silence fell over the class as we sat in darkness slowly burning what we held onto for far too long. Sarita turned and said aren't you going to burn your piece?

I smiled at the permission and wrote quickly on my paper: *loneliness*. In my mind I prayed to myself as the divine energy connected to this body and stated:

"I will no longer carry loneliness around. I will be happy and filled with love."

We put the ashes into a cup, and I promised everyone I would bring it and throw it into the Ganga River.

I directed everyone down for guided meditation. I began to really

love my voice while I spoke. I had gotten so many compliments this

past couple of weeks, it shocked me that something I have disliked so

much about myself was something others found beautiful.

We brought everyone back to sitting around the circle and I read the

English translation for a mantra we would sing together. "That is full,

this is also full. This fullness came from that fullness. Though this

fullness comes from that fullness, that fullness remains forever full."

Sarita sang one line at a time, allowing us to repeat her. She asked

me to read it once more in English. Then we began with joint

movement and warm up. I lead the group with Sarita adding here and

there. We stood and started the traditional Sun Salutation, which was

taught differently in all our classes. This was the sequence and cues

from our textbook, and what Sarita had taught us. She took control of

the class by saying a mantra with every pose, after I had walked through our first flow. Everyone was giggling and chanting along. We did a Moon Salutation as well, adding in the Crescent Moon pose.

We started our group poses, incorporating some pranayama. First was a Roaring Lion pose: Sarita and I sat in Lion pose facing each other, breathed in deeply then rolled out our tongues to let out a large sigh, making everyone laugh. We got everyone into pairs, and I took a video of the class. We also did tree pose, standing with the opposite foot on our legs so that we could support each other by side hugging. We joined our free hands to make a prayer in front of us as well. We then brought everyone around the candles and held each other while balancing on one foot. We ran around the candle and then went back to our mats into Child's pose. Sarita told me we didn't have enough time to do everything on my class sequence. She said that we should be heading into Shavasana now.

We went around massaging everyone while they rested in child's pose, which was a bit awkward for me. Then we let everyone rest on their backs for the dead man's pose. They covered themselves with their blankets and I played a mantra on my phone. We started to massage their faces, neck, and shoulders, then let them rest. Sarita brought out more candles and we made a bigger centrepiece. We slowly brought everyone back up to sitting, and I said my last words of appreciation.

Everyone started clapping and said it was fantastic. Sarita hugged me and then everyone came around, one by one hugging us until we were in a group hug with me in the middle. I had never felt like this before. I had never been at the centre of a group hug. I held back tears. My heart felt so warm and illuminated. I felt so much love in this class.

We all went out for dinner afterwards to the same café I had gone with those two girls before. They had live music, and we all sat down at the same tables. The guitarist was good, and everyone appreciated the songs he was playing. Eventually I looked over at him once he started playing the harmonica, guitar, and a tambourine by use of his

mouth, hands, and foot, respectively. And there it was: the guitar

Miriam had taken that day to the rooftop. I realized I had begun to

believe it was all a dream. That man there was proof that it had

happened, and I took it as a sign that I should not forget what was

experienced; I should believe in the divine power responsible. I knew

that day was me having a conversation with myself through another

body. Earned my trust, saved me from certain death, reminded me

that I can be whoever I wanted to be, and tested my values. My divine

identity spoke to my worldly body through Miriam and I gave myself

permission to be happy.

The morning of graduation the girls lined up on the first floor of

our hotel, waiting to be wrapped in our rented saris. We headed to the

breakfast room, where we waited for the ceremony to start in our

morning classroom (where we had our welcoming ceremony). We sat around the room in an awkward square, leaving space for our mantra meditation teacher. He brought the fire pit and began the fire ceremony. We all took turns throwing flowers into the fire. We sang some mantras and then the other teachers joined us one by one. We moved around to split the room into the 200 hours and 300 hours students, then as instructed, we all took turns saying what we had expected of this experience before we arrived, and what we experienced while being here.

Most of them spoke of friendship – an undeniable connection with these strangers. How they will keep in contact after this and how they have changed because of their friends here. Exactly what I had wished for.

When it was my turn, I spoke without a thought:

"Before I came here, I was fighting depression, and so I came here just trying to find some happiness. While being here I've experienced things that I never thought were possible, and I am so happy to have experienced everything with everyone here. I just feel so loved and happy now." I said smiling while fighting back tears. The girl beside me hugged me, which took me by surprise. That was the first time I had identified my depression out loud, and somehow that made it feel small and vulnerable.

I spent the rest of the day with students, for lunch and dinner. I was finally included.

The next day, I went for breakfast with a large group. We all spoke of what our plans were and when we were going home. My flight was at 5 PM, but my transfer was at 3 PM. I had spent the rest of my morning cleaning my room in the hotel, buying some snacks for my flights, and sitting by the river.

I sat outside on the steps by the Ganga for a while, watching the water slide to the sides and blindly fight the rocks to continue with the current. There was a sweet hum to this giant force slowly sliding by. I lost track of time, staring into the cloudy river memorizing its flow.

I decided to go back to the school to be ready for my transfer. First, I slowly walked down the steps to the water, squatted, and cupped the water in my hands with both hands bringing them together, lifting the water up, and then letting it go – I did this three times, as if I had done this every day of my life. The fourth time I let the water drop but rubbed my wet hands over my face and hair. I got up peacefully and walked up the stairs. I made it to the street when the centre of my chest began to pump rapidly in a panic. A rushing numbness came through my arms and legs. I couldn't control my breath, barely able to inhale. I took two steps before I got a shot of a shivering sensation through my spine from my lower back up to my neck. And then as quickly as the sensation came upon me, everything stopped, and I gasped for air. I continued to walk as I could feel the eyes of strangers on me. I felt light-headed, but more prominently I felt a deep

connection with the Ganga River, like it had just assured me that what

happened this month was something phenomenal and otherworldly.

As if it said, *if you still had any doubts, here is another reason to

believe.*

This place was magical.

On my flight out of Delhi, I watched the most beautiful sunrise I

had ever seen. The mantra for Shiva was stuck in my mind, and I

vowed not to forget this feeling. The sun floated over the clouds,

almost side by side with a crescent moon. I smiled when I recognized

the moon: the moon that Shiva held in his hair. I looked out for a

while then closed the blind so the passengers beside me could get

some rest. I turned my phone on to check some of the photos from

this month, and I noticed a new folder: it was the memory card. I

quickly downloaded the 15 pictures in case when we landed it no

longer worked. I took this as a sign that I had finally let go of the obsession of having these photos and therefore I finally earned them back. Only after temptation, possessiveness and vanity were released and no longer an active energy inside, was I able to receive what was originally desired.

Sure enough when we landed the folder was gone.

Vocabulary

Asana – Body Posture. The Physical movement of Yoga. One part of the 8 limbs of Yoga.

Bandha- A lock or bind in an asana.

Bird of Paradise Pose- Starting in Downward Facing Dog pose, step your right foot in between your hands, keeping the back knee off the ground. Bring your right hand to the inside of the foot, then wrap your right arm through your inner knee and meet your left hand behind your back. Balance all weight onto your right foot and slide your left foot forward, shifting your weight to the left to enable you to stand up while lifting your right leg inside your locked arms. Straighten both legs.

Chakra- An energy circle or wheel within the body. Traditionally there are seven: Crown, Third Eye, Throat, Heart, Solar Plexus, Sacral, and Root.

Chinito – Squinted eyes. Adjective used commonly in the Philippines.

Dhyana- Meditation. One part of the 8 limbs of Yoga.

Diwali- A Hindu festival of lights.

Equestrian Pose- Starting in Downward Facing Dog pose, step one foot in between your hands, bringing the back knee to the ground. Front knee is bent, and weight is spread evenly between front foot, both hands, back knee, and back toes. Gaze slightly up if comfortable.

Ganesh- A Hindu God depicted with an elephant's head.

Half Moon Pose- From Downward Facing Dog pose, step one foot in between your hands, bringing the back knee to the ground coming into equestrian pose. Lift both arms up, gazing up if comfortable. Slight backbend.

Lion Pose- Sit comfortably with knees bent underneath you, and body weight resting on your feet. Open knees apart from each other (to the sides of your mat). Lean forward and place your palms on the floor in front of you, with your finger pointing towards the body. Straighten arms fully and tilt head up if comfortable.

Moon Salutation- A 14-pose sequence which is best practiced at night, especially when the moon is visible. Activates the Ida energy, which is introverted, feminine and responsible for consciousness.

Mudra-A hand gesture that directs energy by forming a closure or seal.

Niyama- Self-Discipline. One part of the 8 limbs of Yoga.

Pranayama – Control of the Breath. One part of the 8 limbs of Yoga.

Pratyahara- Control of the Senses. One part of the 8 limbs of Yoga.

Prayer & Mantrajapa – The meditative repetition of a Mantra or Prayer.

Reclined Butterfly Pose- Commonly referred to as Bound Angle Pose. Starting in a seated position, bend both knees into the chest. Open knees to either side, bringing the palms of the feet together. Once comfortable, support your torso to the ground behind you. Lay down with hands on your stomach or to your sides. Knees can be supported by blocks/etc.

Roaring Lion Pose- Start in Lion Pose with knees apart and palms on the ground. Open eyes and gaze towards your third eye. At the end of inhalation, open your mouth extending the tongue out and exhale producing a steady "aaa" sound from the throat.

Samadhi- State of Realization. One part of the 8 limbs of Yoga.

Shiva- A Hindu God whose name means the "auspicious one".

Sun Salutation- A sequence of poses practiced to warm up the body. It is a complete spiritual practice as it includes asana, pranayama, mantra, and meditation techniques.

Tabo – A dipper or pitcher that is used in Filipino washrooms to wash yourself.

Yama- Social Disciplines. One part of the 8 limbs of Yoga.

"I took my time sitting there watching the odd white-water raft drift

by while their passengers emptied into the river and then screamed to

be pulled back up from the freezing water."

"The sky was a smoky pink mixed with orange, and black birds flew

around in their groups. The contrast of the birds in the sky looked

like a painting resurrected."

"We walked through, letting motorcyclist priority because their honking was just intolerably loud. I was smiling the whole way as we squeezed past the beggars, the tourists and two bulls. I quietly said to myself: 'I miss this'."

"Looking around at the still buildings, knowingly contrasting them with the chaos their walls covered. Life seemed to pause as I soaked the scenery in."

"All I wanted to have was a best friend to talk to: to meet up over tea

and discuss the meaning of life and whatnot. At the very least, I

wanted someone I could count on to come shopping with me or just

go for a walk with. I am just so tired of being alone all the time."

"The light danced through the trees across the river and flicked through my closed eyelids. There were tourists on the bridge down the way whose faint voices carried down-stream. My heart was open and vibrant, my mind was clear and present. I felt at peace, truly. I knew I had to be here, on this rock, on this gorgeous day. It felt like it was written already. "

I hope my experience can help you in some way. I hope it

encourages you to heal yourself, and if you are able, to include

those around you who may seem depressed or lonely. I hope it

opens your perspective on depression. To change the world, we

must first change ourselves. This is just one step in my healing

journey, and I hope to share more with you.

- Kaitlyn J

About the Author

K A I T L Y N   J O N E S

"I will not tell you what I learned, but I would like to share my experience with you for you to find what you need."

Facing depression for the majority of her young life, Kaitlyn finds pieces of happiness while traveling and her relatively new hobby - Yoga. Inspired by a co-worker, she enrolled in a Yoga Teacher Training Course in Rishikesh, India for November 2018. This novel is a memoir of that trip, written and published one year later for her graduation anniversary. Overcoming depression and finding a new awareness and mindfulness, Kaitlyn points back to this trip as the beginning of her second chance at life.